Reminiscences of Two Years in the United States Navy

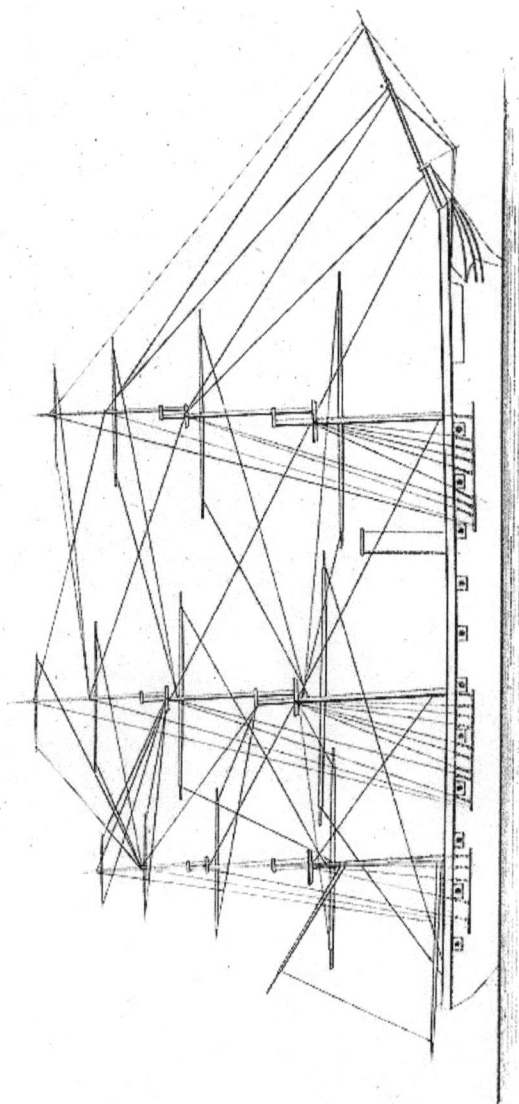

U. S. STEAMER PRINCETON,

(THE SECOND.)

Reminiscences of Two Years in the United States Navy

The Recollections of a Naval Officer During the American Civil War

John M. Batten

LEONAUR

Reminiscences of Two Years in the United States Navy: the Recollections of a Naval Officer During the American Civil War
by John M. Batten

Leonaur is an imprint of Oakpast Ltd

ISBN: 978-1-84677-860-5 (hardcover)
ISBN: 978-1-84677-859-9 (softcover)

http://www.leonaur.com

Publisher's Notes

The views expressed in this book are not necessarily
those of the publisher.

Preface

The only excuse I offer for publishing this little book of reminiscences is that a story half told is better than a story not told at all.

J. M. B.
73 Sixth Avenue
Pittsburgh, Pa.
May 8th, 1881

To the
Grand Army of the Republic,
and to the
Soldiers and Sailors
who gave their lives as an offering for the
preservation of the Union,
and to my mother,
Sarah Batten,
this little book of reminiscences is most
respectfully dedicated.

Reminiscences of Two Years in the United States Navy

After having passed an examination before the Medical Board of the United States Navy, which was in session at the United States Naval Asylum, Philadelphia, Pa., Dr. James Green, President of the Medical Board, I received the following appointment:

Navy Department
22nd March, 1864
You are hereby appointed Acting Assistant Surgeon in the Navy of the United States on temporary service.
After having executed the enclosed oath and returned it to the Department with your letter of acceptance, you will proceed to Philadelphia without delay, and report to Commodore Stribling for temporary duty on board the United States steamer *Princeton*.
Very respectfully,
Gideon Welles
Secretary of the Navy
Acting Assistant Surgeon John M. Batten
United States Navy
Guthrieville, Pa.

After bidding my relatives and friends good-bye, I proceeded to Philadelphia, Pa., and reported for duty on board the United States steamer *Princeton*, which was lying anchored in the Delaware River off Philadelphia, and which was the same vessel on which Abel Parker Upshur, Secretary of State under President Tyler, was killed by the explosion of a monster cannon whilst visiting said vessel, in company with the President and other members of the Cabinet. The duty aboard this vessel was of an initiatory character, to prepare officers for clerical duties peculiar to each of their particular offices. I made the acquaintance on this vessel of Surgeon James McClelland, who was the Surgeon of the *Princeton*. He had entered the United States Navy when a young man, and had been in the service ever since. He was about fifty-five years of age. The first morning after sleeping aboard this vessel, I was awakened by what is always usual aboard a man-of-war, a large gun fired at sunrise. The concussion and reverberation from the report of the heavy gun shook the vessel till it creaked, and, in my half-slumbering condition, I wondered to myself whether it was not a real battle in which the vessel was engaged; but upon mature reflection and inquiry, I learned it was only the report of the sunrise gun.

One day, whilst on board the *Princeton*, a blank book in which were copied a number of choice prescriptions used by many of the old celebrated physicians of Philadelphia, fell into my hands. The book belonged to Surgeon James McClelland. I thought, as I had nothing else special to do, I would occupy the time in re-copying these prescriptions into a blank book of my own; and just as I was re-copying the last prescription, Dr. James McClelland came aboard. He noticed me engaged in writing, and came into the state-room where I was, and observed his book. He immediately asked me where I had got the book. I told him where I had got it.

"Why," said he, "I would not take any money for a copy of those prescriptions. I consider them very valuable, and would not for any consideration let my best friend have a copy of them."

I told him that I believed it to be very wrong not to let prescriptions which have been found valuable in disease, be known. After reprimanding me for re-copying the prescriptions, he cooled down, and became very affable. I, however, got a copy of the prescriptions.

Another day, in rowing aboard the *Princeton* from the United States Navy Yard at Philadelphia, Pa., I acted as coxswain, and came very near capsizing the boat in the Delaware River. The river was very rough, and I got the boat in what the sailors call the "trough of the sea." I, however, arrived on board the *Princeton* safely, after running the boat "bows on" against the steamer. The officer of the deck said:

"Sir, why don't you bring that boat alongside in a sailor-like manner?"

"Why," I said, "I am glad to get aboard in any manner, even though there were a hole stove in the side of the *Princeton* by my boat; besides, sir, I know nothing about bringing a boat alongside in a sailor-like manner." I soon, however, learned to manage a small boat in water very well.

On receiving the following order:

Navy Department
5th April, 1864
Sir:
You are hereby detached from the *Princeton*, and you will proceed to Hampton Roads, Va., without delay, and report to Acting Rear Admiral Lee for duty on board the United States steamer *Valley City*.
I am, very respectfully, your obedient servant.
Gideon Welles
Secretary of the Navy
Acting Assistant Surgeon John M. Batten
U.S. Navy, Philadelphia

I left the *Princeton*, and after bidding my mother fare-well, who was stopping with my sister, who resided in Philadelphia—this was a hard task, and it affected us both greatly; but separate we did, and whether we should ever meet again in this world was a question which time alone would determine—on turning a corner I looked back, and saw my mother standing on the steps of the doorway, weeping. It was to me an affecting separation. I journeyed to the Philadelphia and Baltimore railroad depot, located in the southern part of Philadelphia, Pa., and at 8 o'clock a.m. of a beautiful day I took the train for Baltimore, Md., arriving in that city at about noon of the same day. Having some time to view the city, I took advantage of the opportunity, and promenaded the principal thoroughfares. At 5 o'clock p.m., I took the steamer *Louisiana* for Fortress Monroe, and arrived there the next morning, and as soon thereafter as possible reported to Admiral Lee. On the back of my order I find:

Delivered April 6th, 1864
C. K. Stribling
Commander

Delivered April 6th, 1864
John Calhoun
Commandant
Flagship *Minnesota*
Off Newport News, Va.

Reported April 8th, 1864.—Apply to Col. Biggs, Army Quartermaster at Fortress Monroe, for transportation to Newbern, and then report to Captain Davenport in the sounds of North Carolina.
S. P. Lee
Acting Rear Admiral
Commanding North Atlantic Blockading Squadron

Transportation will be given by first steamer bound for North Carolina.

Herman Biggs
April 9th, 1864

Reported April 14th, 1864.
Report to Acting Master J. A. J. Brooks, Commanding U.S. steamer *Valley City*.
H. K. Davenport
Commander U.S.N.
Senior Naval Officer, Sounds of N.C.

Reported April 15, 1864.
John A. J. Brooks
Acting Master, Commanding U.S. Steamer *Valley City*

It being late in the evening of April 8th, 1864, when I reported on board the United States steamer *Minnesota*, and there being no opportunity to return ashore, I was compelled to remain aboard the *Minnesota* till the following morning, April 9, 1864. Being very much fatigued, I retired early, and soon fell soundly asleep. About 1 a.m., I was aroused from my slumbers by a noise; I could not for the life of me tell from whence it came or whither it had gone; but it was sufficient to arouse and bewilder me, for it made the vessel tremble. I soon arose from my sleeping couch, put on my clothes, and made my way, in the darkness, through the ward-room to the forward hatchway, and to the gun deck. There I found Admiral Lee, with his officers and men, on deck in their night clothes. I soon learned what was the cause of the excitement. It was an explosion of a hundred-pound torpedo under the bottom of the *Minnesota*, which had been borne thither by a torpedo-boat manned by Confederates from somewhere up the James River. The officers and men on deck, in the gloom of the night, were discussing in a subdued but excited tone the possibility of capturing the torpedo-boat; but, owing to the fires in the picket-boats to the *Minnesota* being out, nothing could be done till the steam in them was raised; and in the meantime the torpedo-boat was allowed to return up the James River. The damage to the *Minnesota* was considerable, though no hole was made in her hull. Her guns were dismounted, her partitions were broken down, her doors were jambed, her chairs and tables were upset, and crockery-ware broken. After the excitement of the occasion was over, I returned to my berth, and slept soundly till morning.

After a few days spent in visiting the important places in the vicinity of Hampton, one of which was Fortress Monroe, I took passage on a boat through the Dismal Swamp Canal to Albemarle Sound, and from thence through the sounds of North Carolina to the Neuse River, up which we steamed to Newbern, where I reported to Commander H. K. Davenport, on board the United States steamer *Hetzel*, who ordered me to report for duty to Acting Master J. A. J. Brooks, aboard the United States Steamer *Valley City*, which was lying off Hill's Point, near Washington, N.C., on the Tar River. Dr. F. E. Martindale, Surgeon aboard the *Valley City*, the gentleman whom I was to relieve, met me at Newbern, N.C., and accompanied me to that vessel.

It was 5 a.m. of April 15th, 1864, when I reported to Captain J. A. J. Brooks for duty. I was ushered into the ward-room of the *Valley City* and introduced to the officers, some of whom were not up. James M. Battin, the engineer, one of the officers who had not yet arisen, on hearing my name mentioned, thought that letters directed to him were being called, and he sprang suddenly out of his berth; but it was only to be introduced to a person of the same name, yet an entire stranger. Dr. Martindale had been expecting his relief for some weeks; being anxious to return home to his family, he left for Newbern in the same boat (the *Trumpeter*) which brought us hither from that place.

Washington is a small town, situated on the left bank of the Tar River, thirty miles from its mouth. It was occupied by about fifteen hundred Federal troops. The United States steamer *Louisiana*, the vessel on which the powder was afterwards exploded off Fort Fisher, was lying immediately off the town. Below Washington, N.C., on either side of the river, there was timber. On the right bank, just below the town, was Rodman's Point; three miles farther down the river, on the same side, was Hill's Point, and still farther down on the same side was Maule's Point—places which the Confederates had fortified previous to their falling into the hands of the Federals.

Newbern on the Neuse River, Washington on the Tar River, and Plymouth on the Roanoke River, lie in a circle which might be described from a point somewhere in Pamlico Sound—the former and latter towns being each about thirty miles from Washington, the latter town being in the middle; so that the report of heavy artillery could be heard at Washington from either of the other two places.

Saturday, April 16th, 1864, my diary states that Plymouth was attacked by the Confederates. Firing continued every day till Tuesday, April 19th, 1864, when the place fell into the hands of the Confederates. Lieutenant-Commander Charles W. Flusser made a remark early in the morning of April 19th, 1864, that he would either sink the rebel ram *Albemarle* before night, or he would be in—. Captain Flusser commanded the United States steamer *Miami*, and Captain French the ill-fated *Southfield*. These two vessels had been lashed together at their sterns early in the morning, for the purpose of inducing the *Albemarle* to come between the vessels, and in this manner, if possible, sink her. The rebel ram, early in the morning of April 19th, came floating down the Roanoke River with the current, past the batteries on the right bank of the river above Plymouth, and bore down upon the United States steamers *Southfield* and *Bombshell*, and sunk them. It is supposed that Captain Flusser, in the excitement of the moment, exposed himself unnecessarily, and was shot by a sharp-shooter from the *Albemarle*. When it was noised among the Federal army and naval forces at Plymouth that Flusser was killed, the Federal forces became more or less demoralized, and the place fell into the hands of the Confederates. Captain Flusser was a brave and daring officer. He was interred in the cemetery at Newbern, and on a board that marked his resting place, in the fall of 1864, was inscribed his name, and below it, "Peace to his ashes."

Wednesday, April 27th, 1864, an attack was made by the Confederates on Washington, N.C. There is great excitement among the residents of the place, so that some of them are leaving by every possible route. We hear the firing quite plain off Hill's Point. At 12 midnight. all is quiet. Preparation is being made to evacuate Washington, N.C. The day is beautiful. The ammunition of the army at this point has been put aboard the *Valley City* for the purpose of conveying it to Newbern. The thermometer stands 85°. The Federal large guns on the forts outside of Washington are being fired all day. The *Valley City* got under weigh, proceeded down the river, and shelled the woods below Washington. There were twenty-three shells from the 32-pounder guns fired, which burst among the tree-tops.

Thursday, April 28th, 1864.—This morning there were a few shots fired from heavy guns by the Federal troops, but they soon ceased. The evacuation is going on quietly. The place has a deserted and gloomy appearance.

Friday, April 29th.—The place is quiet. Transport boats are steaming to Newbern, laden with the Federal troops and provisions of the place. Two gunboats, the United States steamers *Commodore Barney* and *Commodore Hull*, steamed up the river to assist in the evacuation. At 3½ o'clock p.m. the *Valley City*, with thirty-one barrels of powder aboard, and a large number of shells, weighed anchor and steamed for Newbern. In going down the Tar River, one of those violent thunder-storms peculiar to that climate came up. It was not considered a very safe place to be aboard the *Valley City* with all this powder during a thunder-storm. I was glad when the storm was over. We got aground for one hour in Pamlico Sound, but arrived safely at Newbern at 9 o'clock a.m., Saturday, April 30th, 1864. Washington, N.C., is evacuated.

Sunday, May 1st, 1864.—The *Valley City* took in coal and then proceeded toward Washington, N.C. At 8 p.m. she anchored off Brant Island light-house. May 2nd, Monday. We got under weigh at 5 a.m., and proceeded toward Washington.—At 4 o'clock p.m. we anchored off Rodman's Point, and fired a shell into Washington at a number of Confederates. We then got under weigh, and proceeded down below Maule's Point, and anchored.

Tuesday and Wednesday, May 3rd and 4th, nothing of note transpired but taking refugees aboard.

Thursday, May 5th, the *Valley City* shelled Hill's Point, then she got under weigh, and proceeded up Pungo River, and anchored for the night.

Saturday, May 7, 1864, the *Valley City* got under weigh, and proceeded to Newbern, where she arrived at 9 a.m. of the 8th. James W. Sands, John Maddock and myself, attended church.

Newbern is a beautiful town on the right bank of the

Neuse River. Just below Newbern the Neuse River receives the Trent River as a tributary. The houses of the place were brick and also frame. They stood back from the street, with yards in front of them, in which choice flowers grew and bloomed. The streets are at right angles. In the cemetery, in the western part of the town, are interred many of the early settlers of the place. The cemetery is very old, and the tombstones, many of them, present an ancient appearance.

On the 9th I was ashore—on the 10th we left Newbern. The 11th we arrived off Maule's Point, and took on as a refugee Mrs. Forbes. The 12th raining, the *Valley City* took aboard some more refugees. On the 13th, 14th and 15th, nothing of note took place. The 16th we destroyed the guns at Hill's Point. The 17th, at 2:45 p.m., we proceeded to Newbern, where we arrived at 8:30 a.m. of the 18th.

The *Valley City* remained off Newbern till June 4th, when we left at 1 p.m., and arrived off Hill's Point at 9¼ a. m, of the 5th. The 6th we went ashore at Maule's Point, and got a mess of strawberries. The 7th we landed at Bath. The 8th two boats' crews were sent to Maule's Point to watch the Confederates, a squad of whom had assembled there. Two shots were fired from the *Valley City*, one to the right and the other to the left of the house on the point. The family living in the house was very much frightened, but nobody was hurt. On the 9th and 10th, nothing of note occurred. The 11th cloudy, the Thomas Collyer, a mail-boat from Newbern, came up with a "flag of truce," and went to Washington.

On the 12th and 13th there was nothing of note took place. On the 14th we went ashore at Bath, and called on Mr. Windley's family. The 15th, we went ashore at Maule's Point, and called on Mrs. Orrell's family. Mrs. Forbes made me a present of a Confederate flag. In the evening, we steamed down to the mouth of Pungo River, and anchored for the night.

Thursday, June 16th.—There was an armed party sent ashore, for the purpose of foraging. After they had returned we proceeded up Pungo River to Leechville, a small place at the head-waters of that river. The occupation of its inhabitants was cutting down timber and making shingles. There was an armed party sent ashore, who captured and brought aboard a quantity of corn. We then left with a scow in tow, and proceeded down the river and anchored off Wright's Creek.

The 17th, the United States steamer *Ceres* arrived from Newbern. An armed party was sent ashore for the purpose of foraging. On the 18th, in company with the United States steamer *Ceres*, the *Valley City* steamed through Pamlico Sound. The *Ella May* soon hove in sight, with two schooners she had captured in tow. On the 19th the *Valley City*, *Ceres*, and *Ella May*, with the schooners in tow, steamed up the Pungo River, and anchored off Sandy Point. At about 10 p.m. we proceeded farther up the river, and landed an armed party of men for the purpose of capturing some Confederates at Leechville. On the 20th we proceeded up the river to Leechville to join the party, which had already arrived there. Three schooners were loaded with shingles. On the 21st, the United States steamers *Valley City*, *Ceres*, and *Ella May*, proceeded down Pungo River with the three schooners laden with shingles in tow. On the 22nd, we anchored in Pamlico Sound. At 8 a.m. we proceeded towards Newbern, where we arrived with the schooners in tow at 8 p.m.

On July 4th, the *Valley City*, in commemoration of the anniversary of the Declaration of Independence, fired twenty-one guns, and a copy of the Declaration of Independence was read to the officers and crew of the *Valley City* by Captain J. A. J. Brooks. On the 5th, the *Valley City* got under weigh, and proceeded towards Tar River, and on the 6th arrived and anchored off Maule's Point. On the 10th, the *Valley City* got under weigh and proceeded to Bath, where an armed force was landed, and captured John Taylor, Company G, 62nd Georgia cavalry. In trying to make his escape, he jumped from a buggy which was drawn by a horse in rapid flight, and in doing so injured his knee, so that he was unable to walk for five weeks. On the fly-leaf of a Bible which I loaned him to read in his leisure hours, he wrote:

> May peace and happiness attend thee, and Heaven's richest blessings crown thee ever more. When this you see, remember me.
> Your most obedient servant,
> *John Taylor*
> Houstin City, Ga.
> July, 1864

At about 10 p.m. of the same day, July 10th, another armed party of men was landed with the intention of capturing some Confederate pickets, but did not succeed. Bath, N. C, is a very small place on the left bank of the Tar River, at the junction of Bath creek, about ten miles below Washington. The place was built of frame principally. The people of the place were rather intelligent.

July 13th.—The *Valley City* got under weigh, and proceeded down Tar River to Durham's creek, and sent a party out to fish; afterwards she steamed down the river, and anchored off North creek, and there brought a boat to, which had permission from the Federal Government to trade with the loyal people of Beaufort county, N.C.

On the 14th, got under weigh and steamed over to South creek; from thence down to the mouth of Tar River, and anchored. On the 15th, the *Valley City* proceeded to off Maule's Point and anchored. Mrs. Daniels and her two children, with her sister-in-law, came aboard. On the 19th, the U.S. steamer *Louisiana* hove in sight. The *Valley City* proceeded to the mouth of the Tar River with her, where we anchored.

After taking abroad our refugees, the *Louisiana* proceeded to Newbern. On the 21st, at 7 o'clock a.m., the *Valley City* steamed for Newbern, where she arrived at 4 p.m. On the evening of July 31st, the *Valley City* was ordered to proceed up the Trent River to guard that river in case of an expected attack. August 4th, the *Valley City* was ordered down to her old anchorage off Newbern. On the 5th, at 8 a.m., we weighed anchor and proceeded down the Neuse River, through Pamlico Sound, and up the Tar River, and at 6 p.m. relieved the U.S. steamer *Louisiana*. At 7 p.m., the *Valley City* anchored near the mouth of Bath creek. Mrs. Quin and Mrs. Harris were brought with us from Newbern, and landed near Bath creek.

On the 10th we weighed anchor and proceeded down the Tar River. At the mouth of Bath creek, two shells were fired from the howitzers, at a house where there were a number of Confederates. At 2 o'clock p.m. we anchored in South creek. On the 11th, at 12 midnight., we weighed anchor and proceeded to Pamlico light-house and anchored. On the 13th, at 4 o'clock a.m. we weighed anchor and proceeded to Brant Island light-house in order to get the mail from the U.S. steamer *Massasoit* that we expected to meet steaming near this point. At 1 o'clock p.m. we weighed anchor and proceeded to above Maule's point, where we anchored at 6 o'clock p.m. On the 18th, at 7 o'clock a.m., we weighed anchor and proceeded down Tar River past Maule's Point, down by the mouth of Bath creek, and down by South creek, where we anchored at 3 o'clock p.m. During this cruise there have been eight refugees taken aboard. On the 19th, we weighed anchor, and proceeded to Maule's

Point. On our way we stopped at the mouth of Durham's creek. Captain J. A. J. Brooks and I went ashore. At 6 p.m. we anchored at the mouth of Bath creek. In the evening there was a heavy thunder-storm, accompanied with rain.

On the 20th, at 9½ o'clock a.m., we were relieved by the United States steamer *Louisiana*, and the *Valley City* was ordered to the neighbourhood of the mouth of Roanoke River, in Albemarle Sound, to join the fleet composed of United States steamers *Shamrock*, *Sassacus*, *Ceres*, *Tacony*, *Chicopee*, *Mattabessett*, and *Wyalusing*, to assist in watching the Confederate ram *Albemarle*, which was stationed at Plymouth, which is situated on the right bank of the Roanoke River, eight miles from its mouth. We arrived at Roanoke Island at 12 midnight, and coaled. A portion of Roanoke Island is a barren, sandy place, separating the Atlantic Ocean from Pamlico Sound.

On Roanoke Island, in 1585, the first attempt to found an English colony in America was made. Though abandoned the following year, it was in advance of any similar effort. After the war commenced, the place was held by the Confederates till the year 1862, when the Federal forces under General Burnside captured the place. On the 21st the *Valley City* left Roanoke Island at 12 midnight., and joined the fleet, and anchored for the night.

On Monday, August 22nd, 1864, at 9 o'clock, a.m., the *Valley City* was ordered to the mouth of Roanoke River, where the United States steamers *Ceres* and *Sassacus* were anchored. We were to take a very dangerous and responsible position, immediately at the mouth of the Roanoke River. During the long dark nights the *Valley City* did not anchor, for it was rumoured that the Confederate ram *Albemarle* might come down any night, and especially a very dark night under the cover of the darkness, so that the *Valley City* must be constantly on the alert. If the *Albemarle* did make her appearance at the mouth of the Roanoke River, the *Valley City* was to fire one gun as a signal to the fleet, which was anchored six miles farther down the *Albemarle* Sound, and then steam towards the fleet.

This Confederate ram was a formidable adversary on water. She had a sharp arrow-like ram extending twenty feet under water in front of her bow. She was plated with iron, which completely protected her inmates from solid shot; she had two two-hundred-pounder Brooke's rifled guns on the inside of this iron encasement, and one port-hole to each of her four sides. She was very unwieldy, but in a body of water like the Albemarle or Pamlico Sound no wooden vessel could cope with her.

Friday, August 25th.—I visited Edenton to-day for the first time. It is situated pleasantly on the bank of Edenton Bay, as it is called, but really Albemarle Sound. The people are kind, courteous, educated, and hospitable. There were magnificent residences in the place, each of which was surrounded by a large yard with shade trees, having that comfortable, spacious, home-like appearance, which so many of the buildings in Southern cities present. When the officers of the *Valley City* first visited Edenton, they were treated very coolly by the people; but gradually they became quite sociable, and we were invited to visit many of the families of the place—in fact, one of our officers afterwards married an Edenton lady. Edenton was a sort of neutral ground, at which the Federal officers and Confederate officers often met. On August 31st, the day was clear and cool. Nothing took place of any note except a false alarm that the ram was coming down the river, causing some excitement aboard the *Valley City*.

Thursday, September 1, 1864, the double-ender *Shamrock* came up from the fleet. Last night some army gunboats took an armed body of men up the Chowan River, to be landed and marched across to Plymouth for the purpose of destroying the *Albemarle*. The project was not successful. The day is cool and hazy. The double-ender *Wyalusing* came up from the fleet during the night. The *Albemarle* ram is expected out to-night.

2nd.—The ram did not make her appearance. The double-enders all went to Edenton. The weather is pleasant.

On the 4th I went to Edenton and spent the afternoon at Mr. B.'s, and made the acquaintance of his daughters. On the 6th, H. T. Wood, paymaster's clerk, and myself, went aboard a tug, and were conveyed to the United States steamer *Shamrock*, from whence we boarded the *Trumpeter*, where Dr. P. H. Barton and myself held a medical survey upon H. T. Wood, and sent him to the United States Naval Hospital at Norfolk, Va. I accompanied him. We left the *Shamrock* at 7 o'clock p.m., in the *Trumpeter*, and anchored at 1 a.m., September 7th, and at 6 o'clock a.m. weighed anchor, and arrived at Roanoke Island at 8 a.m. We left Roanoke Island at 1 p.m., and at 8 p.m. we changed to the Fawn, and after steaming two hours anchored for the night. On the 8th we weighed anchor at 5 a.m., and changed boats to the *Undine* at 11 a.m., and arrived at Norfolk at 1 p.m., when I immediately took H. T. Wood to the hospital. I stopped at the National Hotel.

On the 9th I went to Quartermaster's office at Norfolk to procure transportation to Roanoke Island, but I was a half hour too late, the boat *Undine* having left at 8 o'clock a.m. At 5 p.m. I heard that the *Fawn*, which had made connection with the *Undine* in the Dismal Swamp Canal, and the boat I would have been aboard had I not been too late for the *Undine*, was captured and burned by the Confederates. In the evening I went to the theatre. I passed the time pleasantly at Norfolk in viewing whatever there was of beauty and interest in the place. On Sunday morning I attended service at the Episcopal church, and also in the evening, in company with Mr. Y., of Bellefonte, Center County, Pa. On Monday the 12th, and Tuesday 13th, Mr. Y. and I promenaded the principal streets and visited places of interest.

At 6 p.m., Wednesday, September 14, I left Norfolk in the *C. W. Thomas*, which steamed to Fortress Monroe, where she arrived at 7½ p.m., when I got aboard the *John Farran*, and steamed by the way of the Atlantic Ocean to Cape Hatteras, through the Swash, and through Pamlico sound to Neuse River, and thence up to Newbern, where we arrived at 7 p.m. of the 15th. Having expended all the money that I took with me but a few cents, I felt perplexed as to how I should reach the *Valley City*, which I supposed was at the mouth of the Roanoke River, where I had left her; but on going ashore at Newbern, I soon learned that she was anchored off that place, having steamed there during my absence. I quickly arrived aboard her, feeling delighted that I was once more among my old naval companions. The next thing of interest I learned was, that Newbern was being visited by an endemic of yellow fever.

Having already passed twice through the Dismal Swamp Canal, and would have steamed through it the third time had I not been too late for the boat that was destroyed, but I was destined to pass through it still again on my passage home. Lossing, in his *History of the American Revolution*, in volume I, page 311, gives a very complete description of the Dismal Swamp, through which this canal passes. He says:

Schemes for internal improvements, for facilitating the development of the resources of the country, often occupied Washington's most serious attention. At the time we are considering, he was engaged, with some other enterprising gentlemen, in a project to drain the Dismal Swamp, an immense morass lying partly in Virginia and partly in North Carolina, and extending thirty miles from north to south, and ten miles from east to west. Within its dark bosom, and nowhere appearing above its surface, are the sources of five navigable rivers and several creeks; and in its centre is a body of water known as Drummond's lake, so named from its alleged discoverer. A great portion of the morass is covered with tall cypresses, cedars, hemlocks, and junipers, draped with long mosses, and covered with creeping vines. In many places it is made impassable by fallen trees, thick brakes, and a dense growth of shrubbery. Thomas Moore, who visited it in 1804, has well indicated its character in the following stanzas of his legendary poem, called 'The Lake of the Dismal Swamp:'

Away to the Dismal Swamp he speeds—
His path was rugged and sore;
Through tangled juniper, beds of reeds,
Through many a fen where the serpent feeds,
And man never trod before!

And when on earth he sank to sleep,
If slumber his eyelids knew,
He lay where the deadly vine doth weep
In venomous tears, and nightly steep
The flesh with blistering dew!

'They tell of a young man,' says Moore, in his introduction to his poem, 'who lost his mind upon the death of a girl he loved, and who, suddenly disappearing from his friends, was never afterwards heard of. As he frequently said, in his ravings, that the girl was not dead, but gone to the Dismal Swamp, it was supposed that he had wandered into that dreary wilderness, and had died of hunger, or had been lost in some of the dreadful morasses.' The poet makes him say:

> They made her grave too cold and damp,
> For a soul so warm and true,
> And she has gone to the lake of the Dismal Swamp,
> Where all night long by her fire-fly lamp,
> She paddles her white canoe.
>
> And her fire-fly lamp I soon shall see,
> And her paddles I soon shall hear;
> Long and loving our life shall be,
> And I'll hide the maid in a cypress-tree,
> When the footsteps of Death are near.

Towards the southern portion of the swamp there is a tract covered with reeds, without any trees. These are continually green, and, as they wave in the wind, have the appearance of water. On that account it is called 'The Green Sea.' The eastern borders of the swamp are covered with tall reeds, closely interlaced with thorny bamboo-briers, and present almost an impassable barrier even to the wild beasts that prowl there. Into this dismal region Washington penetrated, on foot and on horseback, until he reached the lake in its centre. He circum-traversed this lake, in a journey of almost twenty miles, sometimes over a quaking bog, and at others in mud and water; and just at sunset he reached the solid earth on the margin of the swamp, where he passed the night. The next day he completed his explorations, and having observed the soil, its productions, the lake and its altitude, he returned home, convinced that the immense morass might be easily drained, for it lay considerably higher than the surrounding country. Through his influence the Virginia Legislature gave a charter to an association of gentlemen who constituted the 'Dismal Swamp Company.' Some, less sanguine of success than Washington, withheld their co-operation, and the project was abandoned for the time.

It was reserved for the enterprise of a later day to open the Dismal Swamp to the hand of industry. A canal now passes through it from north to south, upon the bosom of which immense quantities of shingles and lumber are floated to accessible deposits. By that canal the swamp might be easily drained, and converted into fine tillable land. To every visitor there, the wisdom and forecast of Washington, in suggesting such improvement a hundred years ago, is most remarkably manifest.

Friday, September 16th, 1864.—The *Valley City* left Newbern at 4 o'clock p.m., with Paymaster Louis Sands of the United States steamer *Shamrock* aboard, and arrived at Roanoke Island on the 17th, at 11 a.m., and at 2½ p.m. left Roanoke Island. At 9 p.m. arrived at the fleet, and put stores, which the *Valley City* had conveyed from Newbern, aboard the *Shamrock*.

On the 18th, at 6½ p.m., left the mouth of Roanoke Island to go on an expedition up the Chowan River, and arrived at Winton, on the right bank of the river, at the junction of Meherrin River, at 8 o'clock a.m. of the 19th. Winton was entirely destroyed in the early part of the war, leaving nothing but here and there a wall, a chimney, or foundation wall standing. An armed party went ashore and captured some cotton, and came in contact with some Confederate pickets, with whom they had a little skirmish, or exchange of shots. We left Winton at 4 o'clock p.m., and arrived off Edenton at 9 o'clock p.m., where we anchored for the night. At 7 o'clock a.m. of the 20th we got under weigh, and proceeded to the fleet, where we arrived at 9 o'clock a.m. At 1 p.m. we steamed to the mouth of Roanoke River, where we anchored.

On the 22nd we got under weigh, and at 1:35 p.m. arrived at Edenton. Captain J. A. J. Brooks, Acting Assistant Paymaster J. W. Sands and myself went ashore, and called on Mr. Samuel B.'s family, and spent a very pleasant time. At 3:40 p.m. we returned aboard, and proceeded to our old anchorage at the mouth of Roanoke River. The weather was cloudy and hazy. On Friday 23rd, at 12½ p.m., the ram *Albemarle* made her appearance at the mouth of Roanoke River. We immediately fired our signal gun, and got under weigh, and steamed towards the United States steamer *Otsego*, commanded by Captain Arnold, which was anchored further down the Albemarle Sound. As we passed the *Otsego*, Captain Arnold ordered the *Valley City* to steam as rapidly as possible towards the fleet, and the *Otsego* would follow after. We soon met the fleet steaming towards the mouth of Roanoke River. The *Valley City* and *Otsego* soon fell into line, and arrived at the mouth of Roanoke River. By this time the ram had returned up the river. The fleet remained reconnoitring at the mouth of the river till 6 p.m., when it returned to its old anchorage. The appearance of the ram at the mouth of Roanoke River caused some excitement aboard the fleet, for we were anxious to have the ram come out into Albemarle Sound, so as to have a chance, if possible, to sink her. On the 27th, at 11½ a.m., the *Valley City* steamed down to Edenton, and remained there two hours, and came back to our old anchorage.

On the 29th, at 3½ o'clock a.m., the *Valley City* weighed anchor, and proceeded to and up Scuppernong River. At 11½ o'clock a.m. we got aground in a position transversely across the river, with the stern of the vessel towards the left bank. About seven hundred yards distant on the left bank of the river, in the bushes and wood, a concealed Confederate battery was situated. In making an effort to get afloat, the guns of the *Valley City* were run out of position, the decks were crowded with hawsers and ropes, and the propeller had a hawser tangled in it; so that the steamer was in a very helpless and dangerous position. We were not aware that this battery was situated in the place named till at 3½ p.m. they opened fire on the *Valley City*, and continued firing till half past 5 o'clock p.m. It was some time before the *Valley City* could clear her decks and get into position to bring the guns to bear on the enemy. In the meantime Commodore W. H. Macomb sent orders to Captain J. A. J. Brooks to blow the *Valley City* up and leave her as best we could; but when the *Valley City* got her guns to bear on the enemy's battery, they were silenced at 5½ p.m. The shells and bullets from the Confederate batteries ashore fell around us fast and thick, but fortunately nobody aboard was seriously injured, notwithstanding the vessel was struck several times by shell, and also by a number of bullets. At 9:20 o'clock p.m., after throwing coal overboard, emptying the boiler, and with the assistance of the tug *Belle*, which came up, we got afloat, and were towed by the tug *Belle* down into Albemarle Sound, along side of the *Otsego*. On the 30th the hawser was taken out of the propeller. At 1:15 p.m. the *Valley City* got under weigh, and steamed alongside of the *Tacony* for coal.

I append an extract from the *North Carolina Confederate*, published at Raleigh, N.C., bearing on the brush up the Scuppernong River:

BRUSH WITH THE YANKEE GUNBOATS

The Goldsborough *State Journal* gives an account of quite a spirited little brush between a small detachment of our troops and some of the Yankee gunboats, which attempted to go up the Scuppernong River, in which the Yankees came out second best.

On attempting to ascend the river, two boats were attacked and forced back by Lieutenant Sharp, commanding Captain Pitt's company of cavalry, assisted by two pieces of artillery under Lieutenant Williams of Lee's light battery, and Lieutenant McWaston of the 50th North Carolina regiment, with thirty infantry.

One of the boats got aground at the mouth of the river, about seven hundred yards from the shore, where she was well peppered for some time by both our artillery and sharpshooters, one shot striking her near the water-line.

So hot was the fire upon this craft that the Yankees were all driven from their guns.

Three more gunboats at length came up to their relief, and opened fiercely on our little party, who courageously held their ground and fought them, till the approach of night and scarcity of ammunition admonished us to retire beyond the range of the enemy's guns.

We had three men slightly wounded, and one howitzer was somewhat damaged by a shell.

The enemy's loss has not been ascertained, but it must have been considerable, as their *wooden* gunboat was aground and under the fire of our artillery for some three hours, and it was well ascertained that every man had to seek shelter below from the deadly aim of our sharpshooters.

Hit him again, Colonel W.

Mr. Milton Webster, Executive Officer of the *Valley City*, says of this brush with the Confederates:

It is a pity about that '*deadly aim*,' for we did not have a man injured, and one of the men and myself were over the stern exposed to their guns, and though their shot fell all around us, we were not struck. A pretty correct account of the time of the action and position of the *Valley City* is given, but there was not a man left his station during the action, although their sharpshooters fired at and left marks of their bullets all round our port-holes, and the gangway to which we afterwards shifted a gun to bear on them.

The three other boats did not even get within range of the enemy, on account of drawing too much water. They, however, fired one shot at long range, after the enemy had retired, and this shot was made merely to get the range of the enemy in case another attack should be made on the *Valley City* before she got afloat. One of the two boats they speak of was a tug-boat that went with the *Valley City* up the river to assist her to get afloat in case she got aground, and was manned by two officers—one an ensign, the other an engineer—and five men. The tug-boat was not armed.

It is very singular that they, in their account of the brush, should italicize the word *wooden*, as much as to say we had an iron-clad.

I saved one of their shells that lit on the deck of the *Valley City*, which fortunately did not explode. If the *Valley City* had been afloat, she would have silenced their batteries sooner.

On Saturday, October 1, at 4 o'clock a.m., the *Valley City* got under weigh, and steamed to Edenton. Captain J. A. J. Brooks, Acting Master James G. Green, J. W. Sands and myself went ashore, and visited Mr. Samuel B.'s, and spent the time very pleasantly. At 4 o'clock p.m. we returned to the *Valley City*, and got under weigh, and proceeded to our old station at the mouth of the Roanoke River. On the 3rd, the U.S. steamers *Commodore Hull* and *Tacony* and the tug *Belle* came up and anchored near us. On the 6th, I was ordered aboard the *Otsego*, to hold a medical survey on one of the officers of that vessel, for the purpose of sending him to the U.S. Naval Hospital at Norfolk. When I returned aboard the *Valley City*, I found a refugee aboard, suffering from yellow fever. She was taken to Edenton aboard the *Valley City*, where she died of the disease. We called on Mr. Samuel B.'s family. At 5½ o'clock p.m. we got under weigh, and proceeded towards Roanoke Island. At 12 p.m. we anchored. Early in the morning of the 7th, we steamed to off Roanoke Island, where we arrived at 8 o'clock a.m. On the 8th there was a breeze from the northwest, and the day was clear and beautiful. At 2 o'clock p.m., Paymaster J. W. Sands, Acting Master's mate John Maddock, and myself, with six men, sailed in a small boat to Roanoke Island. There was a heavy sea, and the wind was blowing quite a gale. We landed at Roanoke Island, but did not remain long ashore before we took the boat for the purpose of sailing back to the *Valley City*. We did not succeed. We then took the sails down, and the men rowed us to the vessel.

On the 9th, at 6 o'clock a.m., we got under weigh, and steamed up to the mouth of the Alligator River, where we arrived at 9 o'clock a.m. The *Shamrock* was lying close by. The weather was cold. At 1:30 o'clock p.m., the *Valley City* proceeded up the Alligator River. At 7 p.m. we anchored off Newport News. On the 10th, at 4 a.m., two armed boats' crews were sent ashore on a reconnoitring expedition, but returned at 1 p.m. without accomplishing anything. At 2 p.m. the *Valley City* got under weigh, and proceeded down Alligator River, and anchored at 3 p.m. The weather is cool, and there was frost last night.

Thursday, October 11th, at 5 a.m., the launches were ordered up Frying-pan River. At 10 a.m. I went with Captain J. A. J. Brooks in pursuit of the launches, and after rowing about six miles we came in sight of them. At 2½ p.m. we returned with the launches. At 4 p.m. the *Valley City* weighed anchor, and at 8 p.m. anchored in Albemarle Sound. On the 12th, at 6 a.m., we got under weigh, and arrived at the fleet at 8 a.m. At 9 a.m. we got under weigh, and at 10 a.m. arrived at the mouth of Roanoke River. The ram was expected to come out to-day. On the 15th, at 11½ a.m., the *Valley City* got under weigh, and arrived off Edenton at 11½ o'clock p.m. Captain J. A. J. Brooks, Paymaster J. W. Sands, and Acting Master James G. Green, went ashore. At 5 p.m. they returned, and the *Valley City* got under weigh, and proceeded to the mouth of Roanoke River. The weather is cool and beautiful. At 10 a.m. of the 20th, I went aboard the *Commodore Hull*. At 12 midnight., returned aboard the *Valley City*. At 9½ p.m., the *Valley City* steamed to off Edenton, to protect the tug *Belle*, which had got hard and fast aground during the day. On the 21st I went ashore at Edenton, and spent a pleasant time. I returned to the *Valley City*, when she proceeded to off Roanoke Island, where we arrived on the 22nd at 8 o'clock a.m. At 9 o'clock a.m., Captain J. A. J. Brooks, Acting Assistant Paymaster J. W. Sands and I went ashore, and made the acquaintance of Dr. Walton, of the 103rd Pennsylvania regiment, and Colonel Wardrobe, Commandant of Roanoke Island. I spent a very pleasant time in company with these gentlemen. In the evening I became acquainted with Lieutenant Wm. B. Cushing, U.S. Navy. I will quote a war reminiscence which was published in the Philadelphia *Weekly Times* of June 7, 1879:

by J. M. Batten, M.D., late U.S.N.

It was on the evening of October 22nd, 1864, I first met Captain Wm. B. Cushing. I was then attached to the United States steamer *Valley City*, Captain J. A. J. Brooks commanding. The vessel was anchored about a mile west of Roanoke Island, in Pamlico Sound. Captain J. A. J. Brooks, Paymaster J. W. Sands and myself, left the vessel in the morning, the wind blowing a strong breeze from the west, and arrived at Roanoke Island. The wind continuing to blow almost a hurricane, we attempted to return to the vessel in the evening, but failed; consequently we were compelled to remain on Roanoke Island all night. As I said, it was on this evening I first met Captain Wm. B. Cushing. He then was a young man of twenty-one or twenty-two years of age, wore long, light hair falling around his neck, and was rather reserved in his manners. Captain Cushing, Captain Brooks, Paymaster Sands and myself, occupied a room together that night. The next morning when I awoke, I found that Captain Cushing had gone. Upon making inquiry about him, I learned he had departed at 4 a.m. of the 23rd, in his torpedo launch, a boat he had constructed at the Navy Yard, Brooklyn, for a certain purpose, and had proceeded this far on his expedition with the steam launch.

In referring to my diary, I find that on Friday, October 28th, at 5:30 a.m., the *Valley City* weighed anchor and proceeded toward the fleet. The weather was clear but windy. We arrived at the fleet at 6 p.m. The fleet was composed of twelve double-ender side-wheel vessels, manned, armed and equipped, and commanded by Commodore Wm. H. Macomb, and was anchored about six miles from the mouth of Roanoke River, in Albemarle Sound, and fourteen miles from Plymouth, where the *Albemarle* was stationed. My diary states that at 7 p.m. we got under weigh, and proceeded to the mouth of Roanoke River, where we arrived at 8:30 p.m. At 11 p.m. we were hailed by a voice at the mouth of Roanoke River: Boat ahoy! send a boat! A boat was sent, and the man who had left us so early in the morning of the 23rd of October—Captain William B. Cushing—was brought on board the *Valley City* in his stocking feet, with only a coarse flannel shirt and pantaloons to cover him. He was wet, cold, tired, hungry and prostrated.

My diary states that after leaving us on the morning of the 23rd of October he steamed to the fleet in his torpedo launch, having received from the crews of the fleet twelve volunteer men to accompany him. On the evening of October 27th he proceeded with his small torpedo launch, with a torpedo rigged on her bow, up the Roanoke River. At 3:15 a.m., October 28th, exploded torpedo under the ram *Albemarle* and sunk her. He (Captain Cushing) and another man were the only ones saved from drowning or capture. Captain Cushing, after blowing up the ram, jumped into the river, swam ashore, lay in the swamps near Plymouth till night, then proceeded through the swamps till he came to a creek, where he captured a skiff belonging to a Confederate picket, and paddled himself to the *Valley City*. The torpedo boat was sunk, and about a dozen men were either drowned or captured. In the meantime, the fleet had moved up to the mouth of Roanoke River. Upon learning that Captain Cushing was on board the *Valley City*, Commodore Macomb ordered the riggings of the fleet to be manned, and at the general signal to give Captain Cushing three hearty good cheers; and such cheering—it made those swamps, forests and waters resound with the voices of glad-hearted men.

On the following day, October 29th, at 11 o'clock a.m., the fleet weighed anchor with every man at his post, and proceeded up Roanoke River, the *Valley City* leading, for the purpose of confirming the report of Captain Cushing that the *Albemarle* ram was sunk; and, if true, capturing Plymouth. This is a small town situated on the right bank of the Roanoke River, eight miles from its mouth, surrounded by swamps and large cypress trees as far as the eye can reach. One mile above Plymouth the waters of the Roanoke River divide, one forming the Cashie River, the other the Roanoke River. At about two thirds of the distance from the mouth of the Roanoke River to Plymouth, the Cashie River and the Roanoke River are connected by what is called Middle River, so that these rivers in their course at these points formed a figure resembling the capital letter A, the left line the Roanoke River, the right line the Cashie River, and the horizontal line the Middle River.

The fleet steamed up Roanoke River. The day was beautiful, the birds were singing in the branches of the trees, the leaves of which were gently rustling, and the water could be heard dripping from the wheels of the fleet as they made their slow revolutions. All else was quiet. No man said a word. This was not strange, for we believed the river to be full of torpedoes and its banks lined with sharpshooters. We ascended further and further up the river till we came to Middle

River, when the *Valley City* steamed through Middle and up the Cashie River. The remainder of the fleet steamed on up Roanoke River.

After arriving at a point in the Cashie River opposite Plymouth, we heard heavy firing by the fleet, which continued an hour, and then suddenly ceased. We thought, of course, that Plymouth had been captured. At this point we picked up the other man who was with the expedition, and who escaped. The *Valley City* continued to ascend the Cashie River, and after encountering much difficulty on account of the narrowness and crookedness of the river, we arrived at the Roanoke River above Plymouth, where we could see the town, but we could see no fleet nor American flag. We concluded then that the *Albemarle* had not been sunk, but had driven the fleet back into the Sound. Of course, it was not a very happy feeling to fear the ram might prevent our retreat.

After some delay, and an exchange of shot with the enemy at Plymouth, we descended the Cashie River to Albemarle Sound, where we arrived at 8 p.m., and found the fleet at the mouth of Roanoke River. They had ascended the Roanoke River till they came to some obstruction which placed them at a disadvantage to the enemy; they then descended the river.

Commodore Macomb was now convinced that the ram *Albemarle* was sunk. The *Valley City* was now detached to convey Captain Cushing to Fortress Monroe. We weighed anchor at 12:30 a.m., October 30th, and proceeded through Albemarle and Pamlico Sounds, and into the Atlantic Ocean, and arrived at Fortress Monroe at 7 a.m., November 1. A fleet of about one hundred vessels was stationed there, preparatory to making an onslaught on Wilmington.

Captain Wm. B. Cushing was received on board the flagship with a salute of twenty-one guns, and, of course, was almost worshiped for his heroic achievement. It was at Fortress Monroe I first saw the United States steamer *Kearsarge*, of Commodore Winslow and Alabama fame. My attention was directed to her by hearing an old sailor say, 'Does she not sit like a duck on water?' And truly she did.

Captain Cushing is now dead. He certainly was one of the bravest men that ever trod the decks of a man-of-war. Peace to his ashes! Commodore Macomb is also dead; he died in your city of Brotherly Love, while taking a bath. We all loved him. God bless him.

PUBLISHED IN THE *NEW YORK HERALD*

THURSDAY, NOVEMBER 3, 1864

THE RAM *ALBEMARLE*

Destruction of the Famous Rebel Iron-Clad

The Ram Sunk by a Torpedo

Destruction of the Torpedo Boat

Terrible Musketry Fire

Escape of Lieutenant Cushing

His Adventures in the Swamp

Full and Interesting Details of His
Brilliant Achievement

The Casualties—Etc., Etc., Etc.

Lieutenant Cushing's Official Report
Washington
November 2, 1864
Admiral Porter has communicated to the Secretary of the Navy the following interesting particulars from Lieutenant Cushing, in regard to the sinking of the rebel ram *Albemarle*:

Albemarle Sound

October 30th, 1864

Sir. I have the honour to report that the rebel ram *Albemarle* is at the bottom of Roanoke River.

On the night of the 27th, having prepared my steam launch, I proceeded towards Plymouth with thirteen officers and men, partly volunteers from the squadron.

The distance from the mouth of the river to the ram was about eight miles, the stream averaging in width some two hundred yards, and lined with the enemy's pickets.

A mile below the town was the wreck of the *Southfield*, surrounded by some schooners, and it was understood that a gun was mounted there to command the bend. I therefore took one of the *Shamrock*'s cutters in tow, with orders to cast off and board at that point in case we were hailed.

Our boat succeeded in passing the pickets, and even the *Southfield* within twenty yards, without discovery, and we were not hailed until by the lookouts on the ram.

The cutter was then cut off and ordered below, while we made for our enemy under a full head of steam. The rebels sprang their rattle, rang the bell and commenced firing, at the same time repeating their hail, and seeming much confused.

The light of the fire ashore showed me the iron-clad made fast to the wharf, with logs around her, about thirty feet from her side. Passing her closely, we made a complete circle, so as to strike her fairly, and went into her bows on.

By this time the enemy's fire was very severe,

but a dose of canister at short range seemed to moderate their zeal and disturb their aim.

Paymaster Swann, of the *Otsego*, was wounded near me, but how many more I know not. Three bullets struck my clothing, and the air seemed full of them.

In a moment we had struck the logs just abreast of the quarter post, breaking them in some feet, our bows resting on them. The torpedo boom was then lowered, and by a vigorous pull I succeeded in diving the torpedo under the over-hang and exploding it.

At the same time the *Albemarle*'s guns were fired. A shot seemed to go crashing through my boat, and a dense mass of water rolled in from the torpedo, filling the launch, and completely disabling her. The enemy then continued their fire at fifteen feet range, and demanded our surrender, which I twice refused, ordering the men to save themselves, and removing my overcoat and shoes. Springing into the river, I swam with others into the middle of the stream, the rebels failing to hit us.

The most of our party were captured; some were drowned, and only one escaped besides myself, and he in another direction.

Acting Master's mate, Woodman, of the *Commodore Hull*, met me in the water half a mile below the town, and I assisted him as best I could, but failed to get him ashore. Completely exhausted, I managed to reach the shore, but was too weak to crawl out of the water until just at daylight, when I managed to creep into the swamp close to the fort.

While hiding close to the path, the *Albemarle's* officers passed, and I judged from their conversation that the ram was destroyed. Some hours travelling in the swamp served to bring me out well below the town, when I sent a negro in to gain information, and found that the ram was truly sunk. Proceeding through another swamp, I came to a creek, and captured a skiff belonging to a picket of the enemy, and with this, by eleven o'clock the next night, I made my way out to the *Valley City*.

Acting Master's mate, William L. Howorth, of the *Monticello*, showed as usual conspicuous bravery. He is the same officer who has been with me twice in Wilmington Harbour. I trust he may be promoted when exchanged, as well as Acting Third Assistant Engineer Stolsbury, who, being for the first time under fire, handled his engine promptly and with coolness. All the officers and men behaved in the most gallant manner.

The cutter of the *Shamrock* boarded the *Southfield*, but found no guns there. Four prisoners were taken there. The ram is now completely submerged, and the enemy have sunk three schooners in the river to obstruct the passage of our ships.

I desire to call the attention of the Admiral and department to the spirit manifested by the sailors on the ships in these sounds. But few hands were wanted, but all hands were eager to go into the action, offering their chosen shipmates a month's pay to resign in their favour.

I am sir, respectfully, your obedient servant,
W. B. Cushing, U.S.N.

Rear Admiral D. D. Porter
Commanding the North Atlantic Squadron

The name of the man who escaped was William Hoffman, seaman on the *Chicopee*. He did his duty well, and deserves a medal of honour.

Respectfully,

Wm. B. Cushing, U.S.N.

The Herald Despatches
Mr. Galen H. Osborn's Despatch

Fortress Monroe, Va.
November 1, 1864

The United States steamer *Valley City* arrived at Hampton Roads from the blockading squadron of the Sounds of North Carolina, this morning. She brings the glorious tidings of the destruction of the rebel iron-clad ram *Albemarle*. The terror of the Sounds is at the bottom of Roanoke River. She was blown up by a torpedo early on the morning of the 28th ultimo; and her destruction is due to the personal heroism and reckless daring of Lieut. W. B. Cushing, of the Navy. All the particulars I have been able to collect concerning this feat, which stands prominently forth as one of the most gallant of the war, I hasten to forward for the information of the *Herald*'s readers.

On the night of Thursday, October 27, Lieutenant Cushing, who has on several previous occasions especially distinguished himself, manned a steam-launch with a party of thirteen officers and men, mostly volunteers, and proceeded, under cover of the darkness, up the river towards Plymouth. Eight miles from the mouth of the stream the *Albemarle* lay, surrounded by a pen of logs and timber, established to prevent her destruction by torpedoes.

As he approached this framework, Lieut. Cushing was discovered by the officers of the ram, who hailed him. He gave no answer, the enemy meantime maintaining against him a severe and galling fire, to which he replied effectively with frequent doses of canister. Finding that he could not approach the ram as he desired, a complete circle was made by the Lieutenant, and the launch was again brought fairly against the crib, bows on, pushing back a portion of it, and leaving the bows of the launch resting on the broken timbers.

At this moment, by a most vigorous effort, Lieut. Cushing succeeded in driving a torpedo under the over-hang of the ram, and exploded it. Simultaneously with the explosion, one of the *Albemarle*'s guns was fired, and the shot went crashing through the launch. At the same instant a dense volume of water from the torpedo came rushing into the launch, utterly disabling her.

Lieut. Cushing then ordered his men to save themselves. He himself threw off his coat and shoes and sprang into the water. Several of his men were captured and some were drowned, but I have not been able to ascertain his exact loss. Lieut. Cushing, taking to the swamp, managed to secrete himself from the enemy's pickets, and brought up alongside of the steamer *Valley City* at about 11 o'clock the next night, in a small skiff which he discovered and appropriated on his way.

The steamer *Valley City* brought Lieutenant Cushing as a passenger, and he reported in person to the Admiral the accomplishment of the daring mission he was specially selected to perform. Though much fatigued by the severities of his recent task, he is yet in good health and spirits, and is at this moment the hero of the squadron. He is the same officer that went to Smithville and captured General Whiting's chief of staff, while a regiment of troops was quartered in the buildings on the opposite side of the way. It was he who took a small boat up the Wilmington River, past the forts and batteries, landed and captured a rebel mail, staid three days in the enemy's country, and finally came away in safety with his trophies. But this last act of his stamps him as one of the most daring men in the service. To attack an iron-clad like the *Albemarle*, with a launch and a baker's dozen of men, would seem the height of reckless folly; but to have succeeded in such an enterprise, is to have earned a life lease of glory.

In the affair, paymaster Swann, of the *Otsego*, is known to have been wounded, and master's mate Howarth, of the *Monticello*, captured. Lieut. Cushing speaks very highly of the conduct of all who were with him.

The destruction of the ram was not definitely known until the following day, the 29th, when negroes sent to gain information returned with the glorious news. Reports from other quarters corroborated this intelligence, and finally a reconnaissance by the *Valley City* revealed the *Albemarle* resting on the bottom, with only her smoke-stack visible above the water.

The yellow fever is said not to have entirely disappeared from Newbern, although the succession of sharp frosts in that vicinity has somewhat dispelled it. The steamer *John Farron* left for that port yesterday, taking an immense mail, and a number of officers who have been congregating here for some time, waiting for the sickly season to terminate.

Hampton Roads, Va.

November 1, 1864

The most audacious, brilliant and successful affair of the war, occurred in the waters of North Carolina last week, in which, after the briefest contest, but one as it will prove of the best results, the rebel iron-clad ram *Albemarle* was effectually destroyed and sent to the bottom by a torpedo discharged by Lieutenant William B. Cushing, of the Navy. The great mailed monster that has so long excited the apprehensions of the Navy Department, and held in the Sound a force greatly in excess of that which was usually stationed there, now lies quietly at the bottom of the Roanoke River, a subject of curious contemplation and dread to the fish that frequent these waters. In the squadron every one feels a sense of relief in realizing the fact that the *Albemarle* is no longer afloat, or capable of doing further damage; for it is no secret that she was one of the toughest customers for wooden vessels to confront that has yet floated. Her raid on the flotilla, on the 5th of last May, proved that fact beyond a shadow of a doubt. She then encountered and fought to great advantage three heavily armed double-enders— the *Sassacus, Mattabessett* and *Wyalusing*—and retired, after a long contest, but slightly damaged. While she floated, no post held by us and accessible to her was safe. She could go her way as she chose, in spite of the efforts of our wooden vessels, unless some accident occurred to her which should prevent her steaming. None of the light-draft monitors were ready to confront her, and she threatened to clear our forces out of the State of North Carolina.

Such was the state of affairs subsequent to the

5th of May. Our squadron in Albemarle Sound had been largely increased by the addition of several light draught, heavily-armed vessels; but, even with these, it was somewhat doubtful whether the possession of the Sound was insured us; so it was determined to get rid of the monster in some more expeditious and certain way.

Lieutenant William B. Cushing, a young officer of great bravery, coolness and resource, submitted a project to Admiral Lee, in June last, by which he hoped, if successfully carried out, to rid the Sound of the *Albemarle*, and insure us its possession. Admiral Lee entered warmly into the scheme, as did the Navy Department, which immediately detached Lieutenant Cushing from the *Monticello*, and placed him on special duty, at the same time giving him every facility to carry out the object in view.

Lieutenant Cushing at once proceeded to New York, and in conjunction with Admiral Gregory, Captain Boggs, and Chief Engineer Wm. W. W. Wood, fitted one of the new steam picket boats, which is about the size of a frigate launch, with a torpedo arrangement, and then took her down into the Sound for duty. Having made several reconnoissances up the Roanoke River, which gave him some valuable information, and having perfected his arrangements, on the night of the 27th ultimo he got under way from the squadron off the mouth of the river, and steamed boldly up stream. In the steam launch were Lieutenant Cushing, Paymaster T. H. Swann, a volunteer from the *Otsego*, Master's Mate W. L. Howorth, of the gunboat *Monticello*, and Third Assistant Engineer Stolsbury, in charge of the engine, with a crew of ten men, nearly all of whom volunteered for the service.

An armed cutter of the *Shamrock*, with an officer and ten men, was towed along for the purpose of attending to some of the minor details of the work. It was known that the enemy had pickets along the river banks, and on the wreck of the gunboat *Southfield* sunk by the *Albemarle* last spring, and which lay about a mile below the town of Plymouth. The pickets, who were in the habit of stationing themselves on the hurricane deck of the *Southfield*—the only portion of the wreck above water—were to be turned over to the care of the *Shamrock*'s cutter when the proper time came, whilst those along the river were to be passed in silence, and without giving alarm, if possible.

At about midnight the little picket-boat entered the narrow river, and steamed silently and cautiously up without giving the least alarm. The *Southfield* and three schooners alongside of her, engaged in raising her up, were passed at a short distance—almost within biscuit-toss—without challenge or hail. It was not till Lieutenant Cushing reached within pistol-shot of the *Albemarle*, which lay alongside of the dock at Plymouth, that he was hailed, and then in an uncertain sort of way, as though the lookouts doubted the accuracy of their vision. He made no reply, but continued to press towards the rebel monster, and was for the second time hailed. He paid no attention to the challenge, but kept straight on his way, first detaching the *Shamrock*'s cutter, to go below and secure the rebel pickets on the *Southfield*.

In another instant, as he closed in on the ram *Albemarle*, the rebel Captain Walley, in a very dignified, pompous, studied manner, shouted, 'What boat is that?' The reply was an invitation for him to go to—! Thereupon arose a terrible clamour. The rattle was vigorously sprung, the bells on the ship were sharply rung, and hands were called to quarters, evidently in great consternation and some confusion. A musketry fire was immediately opened on the torpedo-boat, and a charge of canister was fired, injuring some of the crew. Along the dock to which the *Albemarle* was tied, were a large number of soldiers, evidently stationed there to guard against a landing of our force after a surprise; and in front of their lines blazed cheerily up a number of their camp fires, which threw a strong light on the rebel vessel and the bosom of the river. By the aid of this glare Lieutenant Cushing discovered the raft of floating timbers which surrounded the ram on the accessible sides, to guard against the approach of rams and torpedoes; and by the aid of the same light he plainly saw the large body of soldiers thronging to the wharf and blazing away at his boat. To quiet these fellows, he brought the bow of his boat around a little, and discharged a heavy stand of canister into them from his twelve-pounder howitzer mounted at the bow, and sent them flying. Making a complete circle under a scorching musketry fire, at less than thirty yards, he came around, bow on, at full steam, and struck the floating guard of timbers, pressing them towards the hull of the ram. His boat soon lost headway, and came to a standstill, refusing to back off or move ahead. The moment for decisive action had now arrived. The enemy fired muskets and pistols almost in his face, from the ports of the ram, and from the hundred small arms on shore. Several of his men were injured, and Paymaster Swann had fallen severely wounded. The officers and crew of the *Albemarle* cried out: 'Now we've got him! Surrender! surrender! or we will blow you to pieces!' The case looked desperate, indeed; but Lieutenant Cushing was as cool and determined at that moment as one could be under the most agreeable circumstances. He knew that the decisive moment had come, and he did not allow it to glide from his hands. He seized the lanyard to the torpedo and the line of the spar, and crowding the spar until he brought the torpedo under the over-hang of the *Albemarle*, he detached it by one effort, and the next second he pulled the lanyard of the torpedo, and exploded it under the vessel on her port side, just below the port-hole of the two-hundred-pounder Brooke's rifle, which at that moment was discharged at the boat. An immense volume of water was thrown out by the explosion of the torpedo, almost drowning all in the steam-launch; and to add to the peril of the moment, the heavy shell from the enemy's gun had gone through the bottom of the boat, knocking the splinters about in a terrible style. She at once began to sink in the most rapid manner, and Lieutenant Cushing ordered all hands to save themselves as best they might. He divested himself of his coat and shoes, and plunged into the river, followed by those of his men who were able to do so. All struck for the middle of the river under a hot fire of musketry, the balls perforating their clothing and striking all about them, and in two or three instances, it is feared, so badly wounding the swimmers that they sunk before boats from shore could reach them. Lieutenant Cushing heard the rebels take to boats and push after the survivors, demanding their surrender. Many gave up, but two of his seamen were drowned near by him—whether from wounds received or exhaustion, he could not state. Paymaster Swann was wounded and is a prisoner; but how many others fell into the rebel hands has not as yet been ascertained. Lieutenant Cushing swam down the river half a mile, until, exhausted and chilled by the cold water, he was compelled to struggle to the shore, which he reached about daybreak. After lying in the weeds along the river bank for some time, he recovered his strength sufficiently to crawl into the swamp further, till daylight found him lying in the swamp grass, between two paths, and in speaking distance of the enemy's fort. While lying there but partially screened by the low sedge, he saw rebel officers and men walk by, and heard their conversation, which was entirely devoted to the affair of the morning. From their remarks he learned that the torpedo had done its work effectively and thoroughly, and that his great object was accomplished. He did not learn any of the details of the sinking, but heard it stated that the ram had gone down by her dock, and was a complete loss. He also learned of the capture of the paymaster and some others of his crew from the same source.

Finding that there was great danger of his detection if he remained in his exposed position all day, lying within a few yards of two frequented paths, and so near the river, he began to move slowly away towards the swamp. He was obliged to move cautiously, so he lay on his back, and by pushing his heels into the ground, he slowly pushed himself along, and after a long and exhausting effort, passed over the sixty yards of ground that lay between him and better cover. Once concealed, he laid up for the day and rested himself. He was fortunate enough before midnight to get hold of a negro, whom he sent into town to learn the extent of his success. The negro obeyed his instructions, and reported that the *Albemarle* was out of sight—'clar gone sunk.'

At night, Lieutenant Cushing struck through the swamp, and after the greatest and most exhausting toil and pain—as he was in his stocking-feet, and continually plunging over roots, briers, logs, oyster-shells, and lacerating his flesh severely—he reached a point four miles below the town, where he discovered a skiff used by a picket. Watching his chance, he seized this, and, with a single paddle, paddled off to the squadron, four miles distant, which he reached in safety. Only one besides himself—William Holton, a sailor on the *Chicopee*, who had volunteered on the occasion—returned to the squadron. He was picked up by the *Valley City*, the following day, nearly exhausted.

Lieutenant Cushing immediately came here on the special despatch-boat *Valley City*, and reported to Admiral D. D. Porter. To-night he will go to Washington and report to the Department. He is worn out and in need of rest, which we hope he will be permitted to enjoy.

This last brave and gallant action of his is likely to gain him an advance of one grade in his rank, and it will also, if the law is rightly construed, be a great financial success, which is somewhat more substantial. His share of the prize-money from the *Albemarle*, if she is fairly placed at a valuation, would be in the neighbourhood of fifty thousand dollars, an acceptable sum to any one. Lieutenant Cushing has been ordered to the command of the gun-boat *Monticello*, which will await him until his return from a short leave.

The destruction of the *Albemarle* will release the large squadron of powerful light-draught vessels which have, since her debut last May, been maintained in the Sound. They can go elsewhere now.

On a reconnaissance by the *Valley City*, to within

a mile of Plymouth, it was discovered that the enemy had sunk the schooners which were engaged in attempting to raise the *Southfield*, directly across the channel, thus temporarily blockading the river. Although the town was in sight, not a trace could be seen of the rebel ram; and it is proved in other ways, beyond a doubt, that she lies in thirty feet of water, from which it will be impossible to raise her again.

Captain Walley, who had assumed command of the ship only three weeks ago—relieving Captain Cook, who commanded her in the action of May last—began his duties in a very bombastic style. He mustered his officers and men, and assured them that in three weeks he could again attack the enemy and sink and scatter his fleet, and then he would re-take Newbern and drive the Yankees from every foot of North Carolina soil. With the *Albemarle* and their aid, with the co-operation of the gallant army, he would, before the new year, regenerate the state, and leave not a trace of a Yankee within its borders.

It is not improbable that he might have effected a good deal of damage, and perhaps have endangered for the time being our tenure of Newbern and Roanoke Island, as he was nearly ready for his raid. Thanks, however, to the gallant Cushing and his brave comrades, through whose coolness, courage, and skill the *coup de main* was so admirably administered to the mailed monster, all danger has passed, and another destructive blow has been given to the declining rebel navy.

A meed of credit and praise should be awarded to Chief Engineer William W. W. Wood, of the navy, to whose inventive abilities and experience in submarine warfare we owe the contrivance of the torpedo and the successful arrangement by which it is handled and exploded. The one fired by Lieutenant Cushing contained but fifty pounds of powder; but it did its work to a charm. There was no chance of its failing in his hands. The entire arrangement is exceedingly ingenious, and it would be manifestly improper to describe at this time.

The cutters of the *Shamrock*, we omitted to mention, captured four rebel soldiers on picket on the *Southfield*, and brought them along safely to the squadron.

THE *ALBEMARLE*

The *Albemarle* was an iron-clad vessel, similar in general features to the *Merrimac* and *Tennessee*, but much stronger. It is said her iron mail was twelve inches in thickness, and backed by several feet of solid timber. She was armed with two two-hundred pound Brooke's rifles, and was perfectly shot-proof. Her weak point proved to be below. She could have been captured only by ramming, and for that purpose much heavier vessels were needed than any that could be got into the Sound. The torpedo was the only means of destroying her, and that proved successful when tried.

The *Albemarle* is probably the last formidable vessel that the rebels have in the inland waters of North Carolina, and they will hardly have an opportunity of building more.

THE HERO OF THE *ALBEMARLE* IN WASHINGTON

Washington, Nov. 2, 1864

Lieutenant Cushing arrived here to-day, bringing with him the official report of the particulars attending his destruction of the rebel ram *Albemarle*. This act relieves all the sounds of North Carolina from floating enemies, and thus leaves them free to the operations of our fleet. Lieutenant Cushing is a citizen of, and was appointed from, the State of New York. He is satisfied that a large number of lives must have been lost by the blowing up, as the *Albemarle*'s guns were all manned. The Secretary of the Navy will recommend to Congress a vote of thanks, and he will be promoted to a Lieutenant Commander.

After landing Captain Wm. B. Cushing aboard the flagship of the fleet, the *Valley City* the same day, at 2¼ p.m., weighed anchor, and proceeded to Norfolk, Va., and from thence to the United States Navy Yard at Gosport, Va., and was put there on the dry dock for repairs. After the repairs of the *Valley City* were finished, on Sunday, November 27, at 4½ p.m., we got under weigh, and arrived at Hampton Roads, Va., at 6½ o'clock p.m. On Monday, November 28th, at 11½ o'clock, a.m., we weighed anchor, and arrived at Hatteras Inlet at 9½ o'clock a.m., Tuesday, November 29th. At 2 o'clock a.m., on Wednesday, November 30, the *Valley City* arrived at Plymouth, and at 3½ o'clock of the same morning the *Valley City* was ordered to Newbern: we weighed anchor and proceeded towards Newbern. We arrived at Roanoke Island at 11½ o'clock a.m. Our orders were then countermanded, and at 2 p.m. the *Valley City* steamed towards Plymouth, where we arrived at 10. p.m.

During the month of November, 1864, whilst the *Valley City* was absent at Norfolk, the remainder of the fleet, commanded by Commander Wm. H. Macomb, steamed up the Roanoke River, then across through Middle River, and then up the Cashie River to Roanoke River, down which it steamed and made an attack on Plymouth, which, after a hot action, fell into the hands of the Federals. The ram *Albemarle* was soon afterwards raised by the United States government.

On Thursday, December 1, I went ashore at Plymouth, and observed the ram *Albemarle* as she lay at the bottom of the river. At 12:15 p.m., we left Plymouth, and arrived at off Edenton at 2 p.m., and at 4 p.m., the *Valley City* weighed anchor for Roanoke Island, where we arrived at 8 o'clock, a.m., December 2, and at 9½ o'clock p.m. the *Valley City* left Roanoke Island, arrived at Newbern at 1 o'clock p.m., Saturday, December 3rd; Sunday, December 4, I attended church at Newbern.

Monday, December 5; I visited the graves of Captain Charles W. Flusser and Acting Assistant-Surgeon George W. Wilson. The latter died after two hours' sickness, of yellow fever. He was stationed, at the time, on the United States steamer *Hetzel*, off Newbern, and was the surgeon of that vessel when he contracted the disease. He was a young man, and was expecting soon to return North and visit his aged parents, and also a betrothed young lady. They waited, but he never came.

On Tuesday, December 6th, at 4 o'clock p.m., we left Newbern, with Commander W. H. Macomb and his son on board, and on Wednesday, December 7, at 8½ o'clock a.m., we arrived off Roanoke Island. The *Valley City* left Roanoke Island at 12 o'clock m., and arrived at Plymouth at 10 p.m. On Thursday, December 8, at 12½ o'clock p.m., we left Plymouth and arrived at Edenton at 2½ o'clock p.m. We left Edenton at 8 o'clock p.m., and anchored at 10 o'clock p.m., at the mouth of the Roanoke River, where the U.S. steamer *Ceres* and a schooner were anchored. On Friday, December 9, at 9 o'clock a.m., the *Valley City* weighed anchor and proceeded to Plymouth, where she arrived at 10 o'clock a.m.

In the fall of 1864, when General U.S. Grant was short-ening his lines around Petersburg, it was his policy to have every man, both in the army and navy, employed, in order to draw off as many as possible from General Lee's forces at Petersburg. Accordingly, for the purpose of capturing Rain-bow Bluff, the fleet composed of the United States steam-ers *Wyalusing*, *Otsego*, *General Berry*, *Bazeley*, *Valley City*, *Chicopee*, tug *Belle*, and the picket launch *No. 5*, weighed anchor at 5 p.m., December 9, 1864, and proceeded up the Roanoke River, with Commander W. H. Macomb on board the *Wyalusing* leading, the *Valley City* second, and the *Otsego* third, followed by the *Chicopee*, *Bazeley*, *General Berry*, tug *Belle*, and the steam launch *No. 5*.

Commander Macomb was informed by what he sup-posed was reliable authority that there were no torpedoes in the river from Plymouth to above Jamesville, twelve miles up the river. A fortunate occurrence for the *Valley City* took place on our passage to Jamesville. The engine of the *Val-ley City* gave out, and the engineer slowed up and repaired the damage, the *Otsego* in the meantime passing on ahead. By this circumstance the *Valley City* became third, and the *Otsego* second. We arrived off Jamesville about 9 p.m. The *Wyalusing* signalled the fleet to come to anchor, and just as the fleet was slowing up previously to anchoring, we heard a loud report, the concussion of which shook the *Valley City*, which was a short distance off, as if there were an earthquake in the locality. Presently it was reported that the *Otsego* was lost, two torpedoes, one before and the other aft, striking her simultaneously, and sinking her to the bottom of the river. From some fortunate occurrence, the *Wyalusing* had passed safely over the place where the *Otsego* was blown up.

On the following day, December 10, there was found to be a perfect nest of torpedoes in the river off Jamesville, and while passing near by the wreck of the *Otsego*, the *Bazeley* was blown literally to pieces, Captain Aimes, in command of her, and the pilot and also paymaster, Louis Sands, of the *Shamrock*, were in the pilot-house at the time the explosion took place, and were blown with the pilot-house about thirty feet into the air, and alighted in the river unhurt. William C. Rossell, a lad, and John Gerrard, first-class boy, were killed. Captain Aimes then immediately reported to Commander Macomb that "the *Bazeley* is gone up," but by that time she had gone down.

The Roanoke River, from Jamesville to Poplar point, a distance of thirty miles, was dredged for torpedoes. In all, in the river between these two points, the dredging party took up and exploded eighty torpedoes. From Jamesville on, the *Valley City* took the lead, having previously rigged a torpedo-fender on her bow. The river was dredged by means of six boats' crews, each two of which were paired, rowing about twenty feet apart, with a chain suspended between them, dragging along the bottom of the river. Each torpedo was anchored at the bottom of the river by means of a rope, one end of which was tied to the torpedo, the other end to a staple fastened in the centre of the surface of a hemisphere of iron six inches in diameter, resting at the bottom of the river. The rope was sufficiently long to float the torpedo just beneath the surface of the water. The torpedoes were made of tin, each about eighteen inches long and ten inches in diameter, and divided into two separate apartments, one for air, the other for powder. Through the centre of each torpedo, running longitudinally, there was an iron bar placed, extending beyond each end. On the upper end there was a spring trigger, which was held by a light iron cross bar, ingeniously attached to the longitudinal bar, so arranged that from the lightest touch it would fall off, letting the trigger fall on the upper part of the torpedo, striking a percussion cap immediately underneath it in the powder chamber, thus exploding the torpedo.

The boats were protected as much as possible by the *Valley City* following close after, watching the banks of the river on either side. There were dykes on each side of the river, behind which in the undergrowth the rebels often lurked. To obviate this, Commander W. H. Macomb ordered the marines to march a short distance ahead of the dredge-boats on either side of the river; but notwithstanding this precaution, the men in the dredge-boats were fired into, and several were either wounded or killed by the sharpshooters. Sometimes the marines ashore would be driven back. The farther up the river we proceeded, the more numerous the rebels became, and the more our difficulties increased. The men in the dredge-boats did not consider the place a very safe one by any means, and often went into the boats with many forebodings. It was not a desirable place either on the *Valley City*, for there was a constant dread of torpedoes below and sharpshooters above.

Up and Down the River

The *Valley City* left Jamesville at 8 a.m., December 12, and dredged the river, as I have described. In the evening we had proceeded a few miles above Jamesville. I will now quote as I have it in my diary, which was written at that time.

Tuesday, December 13th, at 5:30 p.m., we were ordered back to Jamesville to cover the army. (I will state by way of parenthesis that the army forces at Plymouth, commanded by Colonel Frankle, had promised the fleet their co-operation, but in this the fleet was disappointed.) We proceeded down the river as far as the fleet, when our orders were countermanded and we returned to dredge the river. The remainder of the fleet would lay at anchor, whilst the dredging party, with the *Valley City*, would proceed four or five miles up the river; then the balance of the fleet would get under weigh and steam up to the *Valley City*, and then come to an anchor again; but when the rebels commenced to thicken in the woods along the river, the fleet kept together behind the dredging party.

Friday, December 16th.—We have been dredging the river, and have advanced to within a short distance of Williamston. At 12 midnight. we arrived at Williamston. I went ashore at this place. It is a small place on the right bank of the Roanoke River—the ground rising gently from the river to the rear of the town. The houses are built of frame, and very much scattered. A family I visited there showed me a hole in their house made by a Federal shell passing through it. One of the inmates of the house had been sitting in a chair in a room in the line of the shell, and just a moment before the shell came crashing through the house the lady went into an adjoining room, thus escaping. The chair in which she had been sitting was knocked to atoms. At 1 p.m. we left Williamston, and at 5 p.m. we anchored.

Saturday, December 17th.—We lay at anchor all day. In the morning I was astonished to see a hog swim across the Roanoke River immediately in front of us, because I have always heard it said that swine will not swim. This was the first and only hog I ever saw swim. At 11 a.m. I went ashore to where an old man lived; he was covered with rags, and lived in a secluded spot close by the water's edge. He had no family but a little boy about eleven years of age. There was not even a cow or horse to be seen—everything around him betokened distress and misery. I asked him how long he had been living here. He replied, "I have been living here six years." I then asked him if he enjoyed this sort of life. He answered, "No." I asked him if he had an education. He said, "I can neither read nor write." I then asked if he intended to give his son an education. He replied that before the war he had intended to give his son an education, but now times were so hard that it was barely possible for him to get sufficient to eat. After bidding him farewell, I returned aboard.

Sunday, December 18th.—At 2 p.m. we got under weigh to dredge the river. At 5 p.m. we anchored for the night. The nights are dark and foggy, and the rebel musketeers and sharpshooters frequently come up under cover of the darkness behind the dykes, and give us a wholesome dose from their rifles; but they are soon hurled back again by a dose of grape from our guns. During the nights, to prevent floating torpedoes coming down the river, small boats or skiffs that we had captured from the enemy were tied in line across the river above the fleet.

Monday, December 19th.—The launches that have been dredging the river have been fired into, and Acting Master Wells and two men of the *Chicopee* were wounded. This event caused the rowers to become so much panic-stricken that they dropped their oars, lay down in the bottom of the launches, and allowed their boats to float down with the current. It was with much difficulty that Captain J. A. J. Brooks, by calling to them from the *Valley City*, could get them aroused; but finally they came alongside. We, however, kept on dredging the river till we came to a point in the Roanoke River, where we anchored. The river at this point where the fleet is anchored makes a bend like that of a horseshoe. The ground on the inside of the bend, on the right bank of the river, is low and level, and covered with young saplings or undergrowth. At the heels of this horseshoe bend ran a high ridge, covered partly with pop-lar trees and partly with white-oak trees. The fleet lay on the Plymouth stretch of the river, or near stretch, and at the end of the far stretch where the river runs under the high bluff, the rebels, as we ascertained afterwards, had fortified with artillery, and an army said to be ten thousand strong. We did not then suspect we would find the rebels in force, till we got to Rainbow Bluff. This place was known by the name of Poplar Point.

All the fleet was at anchor, and had been since 3 o'clock p.m. The day was beautiful. The fish were nibbling at piec-es of hard tack which had been thrown overboard by the sailors. The current of the river rushed swiftly past, mak-ing the rudder flap in the water. The men were lounging about on the berth deck, resting. The cook was preparing supper, the messenger boys were carrying victuals from the galley to the ward-room, and placing them on the table. The officer of the deck was pacing to and fro on the star-board side of the vessel. Captain Brooks was in his cabin. Many of the officers were in the ward-room. All else was quiet. I was pacing the port side of the *Valley City*. Pilot John A. Lewis was standing on the after hatchway, a little above the gun-deck amidships. As I approached him in walking from the bow of the vessel towards him, I said to him, "Pilot, what do you think of the prospect of getting to Rainbow Bluff?" He replied, "I think we will get there by and by, if we have patience and the rebels don't blow us up." Just as I was turning to pace to the bow of the *Valley City*, I heard a report ashore like that of a number of bar-rels of fire-crackers exploding. Simultaneously with this explosion, I heard the zipping of bullets in the air close to my head, and striking the bulwarks of the vessel close by me. Then artillery fire commenced.

In the meantime three loud and prolonged rattles were

sprung by the officer of the deck, calling all hands to quarters. I ran down the forward hatchway and through the berth-deck to the dispensary, which was my station, and which was just in front of the boiler on the berth-deck, and at the foot of the steps of the hatchway on which John A. Lewis was standing when the firing commenced. He was passed down to me, killed by a bullet from a sharpshooter, passing through his head from ear to ear. John A. Lewis was pilot of the ill-fated *Otsego*, and had been ordered aboard the *Valley City* for general duty after the sinking of that vessel. At the time that pilot John A. Lewis was killed, I had my full officer's uniform on, but he had on a blouse and soft felt hat. I felt certain at the time that the ball that killed John A. Lewis was intended for me, as I was nearly in line of the shot.

The rebels made it pretty warm for us from 5 to 9 o'clock p.m. The *Valley City* was struck three times with shell, and fired one hundred and thirty-six shots. One of the shells that struck the *Valley City* came into a lamp-closet just over my head and near the end of the boiler, but did not explode. An old sailor sitting near by where I was standing, upon seeing the ceiling broken above my head, said, "Don't be alarmed; lightning nor shells never strike twice in the same place." Another shell went crashing through the ward-room, down through an old family Bible (which Acting Ensign Milton Webster had captured ashore), and then out of the ward-room through a passage-way in which some negroes off the *Otsego* were lying concealed, killing them, and then exploding in the river. In the meantime, the remainder of the fleet kept up a constant fire.

During the battle, Acting Ensign Milton Webster performed some acts of daring, by taking the end of a hawser in a cutter, manned by negroes, ashore, and making it fast to a tree, under a shower of bullets and shells. The cutter was pierced several times with bullets, but nobody in it was hurt. The hawser was made fast to the tree for the purpose of drawing the stern of the *Valley City* around so as to bring her guns to bear on the enemy.

After a brisk fire from the fleet for four hours, the rebels ceased firing, but annoyed the fleet during the night by squads of infantry firing from behind the dykes and then running away. It was dangerous to have a light aboard the vessel, and we were therefore compelled to take our suppers as best we could in the dark.

Tuesday, December 20th.—We are engaged in burying the dead and skirmishing with the enemy, the rebels with their accustomed barbarity firing on the burying party. We were annoyed all day by the sharpshooters and batteries of the enemy, but continued to hold our own and to keep the enemy back.

On Wednesday, December 21, the *Valley City* weighed anchor at 2:10 o'clock p.m. The Confederates were firing musketry at the *Wyalusing*. At 2:40 p.m. the *Valley City* steamed ahead, around the turn which opened up the far stretch of the river. This stretch of the river was covered by rebel artillery. The *Valley City* had scarcely showed her bow around the turn, till she received a severe shot from the rebel batteries, which plunged diagonally through the pilot-house, which was lined outside with half-inch iron, knocking off the door thereto, wounding three men—the pilot John A. Wilson, Charles Hall, and John Wood: the latter two were mortally wounded. The *Valley City* immediately dropped out of range of said battery, and came to anchor at 3:05 p.m. In the evening the fleet dropped farther down on the near stretch of the river. The *Valley City* lost her torpedo-fender.

December 22nd.—Last night we were again annoyed by

musketry and sharpshooters ashore. During the day, after burying the dead, the *Valley City* dropped down below the fleet to arrange on her bows another torpedo-fender. About 2:20 p.m. we heard loud whistling from steam launch *No. 5*, which was bringing up the mail from Plymouth. I was standing on the poop-deck, and through the bushes on the flat on the inside of the bend I saw a regiment of rebels running towards the launch, at the same time keeping up a rapid fire at her. The *Valley City* dropped her torpedo-fender, steamed down, and after firing a few shots of grape at the rebels, they retreated. In the meantime, Commander W. H. Macomb learned that the rebels had been removing their batteries that commanded the far stretch of the river to a point below us, so as to command the near stretch, and if possible prevent our returning down the river, and thereby capture the fleet. Matters were becoming desperate, and Commander Macomb therefore determined to retreat down the river. The *Valley City* was the first to go by the rebel batteries, the remainder of the fleet keeping up a rapid fire at them. The current of the river was so strong, and the bend under the rebel batteries so sharp, that the *Valley City* whirled round like a water-wheel, first striking the bow against the shore, and then the stern. I was fearful we might be boarded. An attempt was also made to fell trees on the fleet whilst passing. After the *Valley City* had passed safely by the rebel batteries, she came to anchor, trained her guns on the enemy, and in conjunction with the remainder of the fleet above the bend of the river, kept up a rapid fire whilst a second vessel passed; and thus one vessel of the fleet after another passed safely around the turn of the river, under fire of the rebel batteries.

Commander Macomb now gave the *Valley City* orders to proceed down the river cautiously, and have the river dredged in our rear. For a short distance Captain J. A. J.

Brooks had the men in cutters, dredging the river; but after consulting his executive officer, Milton Webster, Acting Assistant Paymaster J. W. Sands and myself, as to the propriety of steaming down the river without dredging it, it was agreed upon to call the dredge-boats in, and we proceeded down the river, shelling the woods on right bank of the river and then came to an anchor above Williamston.

Friday, December 23rd.—The *Valley City* continued steaming down the river, and anchored off Williamston at 12 midnight. At 1 p.m. she weighed anchor and steamed to off Jamesville, where she arrived at 5 p.m., the remainder of the fleet following close in our rear.

On Saturday, December 24, the *Valley City* proceeded two miles up the river to tug the *Chicopee* off, which had got transversely across the river, preventing the fleet behind her from descending. The *Valley City* returned and anchored off Jamesville at 10 o'clock a.m. The fleet is all now anchored off Jamesville, and is engaged in destroying the wreck of the *Otsego*. During this expedition I never had my clothes or shoes off.

On Thursday, December 29th, at 11½ o'clock a.m. the *Valley City* weighed anchor and proceeded to Plymouth, where we arrived at 12½ p.m.

THE NEW YORK HERALD
JANUARY 9, 1865, NEWBERN
ADDITIONAL DETAILS OF THE EXPEDITION
UP ROANOKE RIVER
THE FLEET REACHES POPLAR POINT

From Our Newbern (N.C.) Correspondent.
Newbern, N.C. December 27, 1864
The expedition that left Plymouth, N.C., on the 9th instant, has returned and anchored off Jamesville,

Roanoke River, having by arduous labour accomplished results that reflect great credit upon the commanding officer and his subordinates.

ORGANIZATION OF THE EXPEDITION

The naval portion of this expedition sailed from Plymouth on the evening of the 9th instant, in the following order: *Wyalusing*, Lieutenant Commander Earl English, bearing the broad pennant of Commander W. H. Macomb, commanding the fourth division of the North Atlantic squadron; *Valley City*, Acting Master J. A. J. Brooks; *Otsego*, Commander Arnold; *Chicopee*, Commander Hannell; *Bazeley*, Acting Ensign Aimes; tug *Belle*, Acting Master Green; and the picket launch *No. 5*, Acting Ensign Chapman. The *Shamrock* was to follow.

A land force commanded by Colonel Frankle had started from Plymouth at daylight the same morning, to co-operate with the fleet.

THE *OTSEGO* DESTROYED BY A TORPEDO

Without interruption, the squadron at 9 o'clock the same night arrived at Jamesville, a small town above Plymouth some twelve miles, when the signal to anchor was made from the flag-ship. The night being dark, and the river flowing rapidly in its narrow and tortuous channel, it was thought best to proceed no further until daylight. The *Wyalusing* had just let go her anchor a few yards above the town, when two loud reports were heard astern, and dense volumes of smoke and steam were seen to envelop the *Otsego*. That fine vessel had struck two torpedoes, one under the port coal-bunker, the other beneath the keelson, driving a large hole through her bottom, and throwing one of her hundred-pounder rifled Parrotts into the air. She sank in fifteen minutes in three fathoms of water, being a complete wreck. Her officers and men lost all their clothing, except what they had on at the moment of the explosion, but were cared for by their comrades of the other vessels, who hurried to their rescue, and periled their own lives in saving their shipwrecked fellow-sailors. Commander Arnold behaved with great coolness, and his self-possession soon restored order and discipline on board the sunken ship, or rather on her hurricane deck, which alone remained out of water.

Destruction of the *Bazeley*

In the morning orders were given to drag for torpedoes, when it was found that the *Otsego* had struck upon a perfect nest of them. The boats which had been passing and repassing to and from her during the night, had rowed over numbers of them, happily without touching them. Several were picked up alongside the *Otsego*, and two were hanging to the torpedo-fender rigged at her bow. The steamer *Bazeley* during the morning was ordered to run down to Plymouth, to convey orders and dispatches, taking on board for that purpose Paymaster Louis Sands, of the *Shamrock*, who had been detailed as one of Commander Macomb's aids in this expedition. On her way down, being directed to communicate with the *Otsego*, Captain Aimes ran towards the sunken vessel, when a torpedo struck the *Bazeley* under the pilot house, blowing a hole clear through her, killing Wm. C. Rossell, a lad, and John Gerrard, first-class boy, and sinking the ship instantly. The officers and remainder of the crew escaped by swimming, and were picked up by boats. Captain Aimes, upon returning to the flagship, thus laconically reported his loss to Commander Macomb: "Sir, the *Bazeley* has gone up."

The destruction of two of our vessels so quickly made things look blue, but the grit and metal that headed the expedition were sufficient to overcome such disasters.

A Fresh Start

Preparations were now fully carried out to drag the river by boats for the torpedoes, which were constantly found in the richest and choicest clusters, in some places eight or nine being placed across the river in a line, and having susceptibilities of the most sensitive nature, going off on the slightest provocation. Communication with Plymouth having been obtained, the signal was made to advance, the *Valley City* taking the lead.

Mr. Chamberlain, a civilian, had volunteered to go with the expedition with a calcium light, which proved to be of great advantage to the fleet in the intense darkness of the nights. The light was placed on the leading vessel, and made our pathway as clear as broad daylight. The fleet proceeded slowly, having six boats constantly employed in dragging and picking up torpedoes, which continued to be found in great profusion. Large numbers were found at Shad Island Bend and other points, and many exploded in the attempt made to get them on shore. Eighty were taken up in a distance of thirty miles.

Living On the Enemy

The fleet anchored off several of the plantations along the river, and the men were allowed to regale themselves with fresh provisions and other luxurious articles that were contraband of war. All articles of military value were taken or destroyed, and a quantity of cotton pressed into the service as bulwarks against the sharpshooters who lined the banks of the stream. Mr. Speller, a rich planter, owning a place called Speller's Landing, was arrested and sent to Plymouth. He had accepted a nomination to a seat in the rebel Legislature, had three sons in the rebel army, and was himself a bitter reviler and opponent of the government. Other prominent rebels were also seized and sent to Plymouth. One of them offered Commander Macomb and Lieutenant Commander English a large amount of gold, which he had on his person, to release him; but like Paulding and Van Wert of old, the patriotism of the sailor chiefs revolted at the attempt to bribe them, and an order to place the rebel in closer confinement was the only result of the proposition. Corruption has been little known in this war among our naval officers; and though many of them are far from wealthy, their honour and good name are more precious in their eyes than millions of dishonourable wealth.

THE OPERATIONS OF THE ARMY

It was part of the programme that Colonel Frankle should communicate with the fleet at Jamesville; but without waiting for the arrival of the vessels, he pushed on his men to Foster's Mills, where a skirmish ensued with the enemy, who were repulsed. The mills were burned, and Colonel Clark was left to hold the place, while the main body proceeded onward, the rebels retreating on Rainbow Banks, a very strong and commanding position on the river, twenty miles above Williamston. The fleet learned the news by one of Colonel Clark's scouts, and the next day one of our picket boats, which had been sent back to Jamesville, returned to the fleet, bringing additional intelligence that the army, getting out of provisions, had fallen back to Jamesville. Commander Macomb sent a dispatch to Colonel Frankle commanding, stating that time was precious; that the fleet would proceed at all hazards, and would turn back for nothing until it reached the bluff; and urging that the troops should go forward at once. A promise was returned that the troops would again move forward in a short time.

The Fleet Approaches Poplar Point

The fleet kept on its way for several days more, dragging the river at every step, exploding torpedoes, fighting sharpshooters, and pressing forward toward Rainbow Bluff; until, on the evening of the 20th, we turned a bend in the stream exposing to view Poplar Point, a high bluff thoroughly commanding the river.

The Marines on Shore Duty

On our left, after doubling the bend, was a large marshy plain protected by a dyke, behind which sharpshooters were thought to be lurking. Commander Macomb ordered the marines of the squadron to land, and under command of Acting Ensign Fesset, of the *Wyalusing*, to move along the bank, behind the levee, and look out for the enemy. They soon found the rebel pickets and skirmished with them, the rebels being driven back towards the point. Soon a large body of rebels was found, and a brisk little action took place. A prisoner being captured by Sergeant Kane, of the *Shamrock*, belonging to Whitford's rebel regiment, reported that his regiment was in the swamp, as the advance of the rebels, whose entire strength was some six thousand men. The marines continued the skirmishing until nightfall, when they were recalled, having throughout the day behaved admirably, retaining the good reputation which that branch of the service has always held.

THE *VALLEY CITY* ENCOUNTERS A BATTERY

No sooner had the *Valley City*, which continued to be the leading vessel, shown her head around the point, than she was saluted by a battery which the rebels had placed there so skilfully as to give them accurate and deadly aim. She replied with great effect, and silenced the battery; but night fell, and the firing ceased. During the night all the vessels were annoyed by the rebels, who would sneak up under cover of the trees, fire a volley upon our decks, and skedaddle, their retreat being often accelerated by a wholesome dose of grape. During the day the *Valley City* had suffered badly from the rebel battery. Pilot John A. Lewis was shot through the head with a Minie ball and instantly killed. He was buried on the bank of the river—the rebels, with their accustomed barbarity, firing on the burying party.

A shell exploded in the pilot-house of the *Valley City*, badly wounding her other pilot. A number of her men were also badly hurt.

THE FLEET IN A TIGHT PLACE

The 21st and 22nd were passed in shelling the batteries on Poplar Point, and endeavouring to drag the river for torpedoes, that were now thicker than ever. As fast as our boats would leave the ships to commence dragging, the rebels would open on them, wounding and killing the men. A new battery opened on the *Valley City*, inflicting serious damage on her. The other ships, with their hundred-pounder rifles, drove the rebels off repeatedly, but only to return whenever our fire slackened. It was plain that we could no longer do without a land force to drive the fellows off and clear the way for our dragging boats. Every moment the rebels thickened in the woods; the trees and bushes were alive with sharpshooters; batteries were discovered in process of erection in our rear; and in a word, the position of the squadron was critical.

The Fleet Withdraws to Jamesville

Commander Macomb again sent a despatch to the colonel commanding the land forces, begging him to press forward without delay. The reply was that the army would advance when transportation permitted. The position of the fleet was untenable for twenty-four hours more; to have remained would have insured the loss of another vessel; to advance was impossible without army co-operation: so, very reluctantly, Commander Macomb gave the order to fall back to Jamesville, there to await the action of the army. The fleet fought its way back for seven or eight miles, and the rest of the way was passed in quiet.

The *Otsego* had not yet been put out of commission—Commander Arnold and a portion of her crew remaining on her hurricane-deck, and living *al fresco*. Her heavy battery had been removed to the *Shamrock* and *Wyalusing*, but her brass howitzer still remained on her hurricane-deck to defend her crew. A survey was now held upon her, and it was decided that it was impossible to raise either her or the *Bazeley*. Everything that could be removed was taken away, and two torpedoes were placed in her hull and exploded, thus finishing the work of the rebels. Her remains were then set on fire, and she was burned to the water's edge.

The entire fleet, with the exception of the *Chicopee* and *Mattabessett*, are now at Jamesville; and the United States steamer *Lockwood*, to which Captain Aimes was ordered after the loss of the *Bazeley*, joined it last night, having sailed from Newbern to do so.

COMMANDER MACOMB

The indomitable perseverance of Commander Macomb and his captains, in pushing on through a river filled with torpedoes and lined with sharpshooters for fifty miles, dragging almost every foot of the way, and driving the enemy before them, is unsurpassed even in the brilliant naval history of this war. Many commanders would have faltered after losing two of their vessels; but there was no faltering in Macomb. It was not until all hope of land co-operation was exhausted, and until it was demonstrated that without a land support he could go no further, that he consented to retire. Throughout the whole expedition, he asked his men to encounter no danger that he did not himself share. His exposure of himself to death was constant and unflinching; his coolness and self-possession never left him; and in him his officers and men beheld an example worthy of their emulation.

Thanks of the officers of the *Otsego*, to Captain Wood and officers of the transport, *General Berry*:

WRECK OF UNITED STATES STEAMER *OTSEGO*

Roanoke River, N.C.

December, 15, 1864

The officers of this vessel desire to express their thanks to Captain Wood and other officers of the army transport, *General Berry*, for the politeness and kind consideration they received on board that boat, after their own vessel was blown up by torpedoes, on the night of December 9, and the polite manner in which they furnished both officers and men with every facility for obtaining the comforts they so much needed.

H. N. T. Arnold, Lieutenant Commander
Henry D. Foster, Ensign and Executive Officer
J. P. Gallagher, Ensign
Wm. H. Mclean, Ensign
George C. Reynolds, Assistant Surgeon
Samuel C. Midlam, Acting First Ass't Engineer
R. A. Rolfe, Captain's Clerk
Robert S. Houston, Paymaster's Clerk
Franlin Stedman, Acting Master's Mate

THAT OLD FAMILY BIBLE

A Bible captured near Windsor, North Carolina, during the expedition up Roanoke River, on the night of December 16th, 1864, by Ensign Milton Webster, on a marauding expedition, is over a hundred years old, as is shown by its title-page: "Edinburgh: Printed by Alexander Kincaid, his Majesty's Printer, MDCCLX-IX." The book originally belonged to W. A. Turner, of Windsor, North Carolina, as that name appears in gilt upon one of the corners of the Bible; and on a page in the book appears the following record:

David Turner and Elizabeth Armistead were married Tuesday, August 16th, 1785.

David Turner born September 2nd, 1738; Elizabeth Armistead born December 29th, 1759.

Thomas Turner born July 18th, 1786, 4:30 afternoon; William Armistead Turner born December 13th, 1787, nine o'clock a.m. They were both baptized Sunday, August 2nd, 1789, by the Rev. McDowell.

George Turner born November 24th, about 5 o'clock in the morning, 1789, and baptized Sunday, twenty-first of February following, by the Rev. W. Blount.

Sarah Turner born April 28th, fifty minutes after nine in the morning, 1791, and baptized November 27th, same year, by Rev. W. Wilson.

Mary Turner born November 8th, at eight o'clock in the morning, 1793, and baptized June 4th following, by Rev. Mr. Petigro, and died August 8th, 1794, some time between three and four o'clock, which was before day.

Hannah Turner born October 17th, about eleven o'clock in the morning, 1796, and was baptized second Sunday in July following, by the Rev. W. Joseph Gurley.

George Turner departed this life August, 1801.

David Turner was born September 2, 1738, and died May 17th, 1802, in the 64th year of his age.

My dear little Sarah and Hannah Turner both departed this life March 15th, 1805.

Elizabeth Turner departed this life May 17, 1822, aged 62 years, 4 months and 18th days.

Thomas Turner died on the 6th day of January, 1847.

All the forenamed persons, with the exception of the writer hereof, are buried in the grave-yard at the plantation whereon the father, David Turner, and family lived, two and one-half miles west of the town of Windsor.

No doubt the writer of the above is also dead, and time and the chances of war may have scattered any remaining members of the family.

THE *VALLEY CITY* AND HER OFFICERS

The officers of the U.S. Steamer *Valley City* were as follows:

Acting Master Commanding
John A. J. Brooks

Acting Ensign and Executive Officer
Milton Webster

Acting Master's Mates
Charles F. O'Neill and John Maddock

Acting Assistant Paymaster
J. Woodville Sands

Acting Assistant Surgeon
John M. Batten

Engineers—Second Assistant in charge
James M. Battin

Engineers—Acting Third Assistant
John Minton

Acting Master and Pilot
John A. Wilson

Captain J. A. J. Brooks was a North Carolinian by birth, and was acquainted with the waters and people of North Carolina. He was a full-sized man of fine figure, 35 years of age, brown piercing eyes, light hair, and in general appearance a fine-looking officer. He was brave, and ever on the alert. Many nights whilst the *Valley City* was laying at the mouth of Roanoke River watching for the rebel ram *Albemarle*, I found

Captain Brooks at all hours on deck—I often wondered when he slept. In battle he was cool and brave. Under his command the *Valley City* was considered, by the Confederates in that vicinity, a terror to the waters of North Carolina.

It was on the *Valley City*, whilst in a fight at Elizabeth, N.C., a man sat over the opened end of a barrel of powder to prevent it from being ignited, after an enemy's shell had entered and exploded in the powder magazine, and thus saved the vessel. The man was immediately promoted to a gunner.

At many places to which the *Valley City* steamed, Captain Brooks would be anxious to ascertain how many Confederates there were in the locality. Upon asking some coloured people, who were always assembled to greet us, how many rebels there were at a certain locality, they would make the following reply: "I don't know, sah; but dar is a right smaht number dar." Upon pressing them for a more definite answer they would repeat, "I don't know, massa; but dar is a right smaht number dar."

The *Valley City*, and I believe all naval vessels, were directed to go ahead, fast, slow, or stop, or back fast or slow, by a bell hung in the engine room connected with the pilot-house by a wire which was pulled by the pilot. One bell was to start; two bells, go ahead slow; four bells, go ahead fast; and one bell to stop (that is when the vessel was in motion); three bells back; two bells, back slow; and four bells, back fast.

The time of day was noted by means of a bell, as follows: One bell, 12½ o'clock, p.m.; two bells, 1 o'clock, p.m.; three bells, 1½ o'clock, p.m.; four bells, 2 o'clock, p.m.; five bells, 2½ o'clock, p.m.; six bells, 3 o'clock, p.m.; seven bells, 3½ o'clock, p.m.; and eight bells, 4 o'clock, p, m.; then, one bell, 4½ o'clock, p.m., and so on till 8 o'clock, p.m.; then, one bell, 8½ o'clock, p.m., and so on till 12 o'clock, p.m.; thus the time during the first twelve hours of the following day was noted, and in the same way any succeeding twelve hours.

Each watch remained on duty four hours, say from 12 o'clock m. until 4 o'clock p.m., when it was relieved by another watch, which would remain on duty until 8 o'clock p.m., when this watch was again relieved by another watch, which would remain on duty four hours, or until 12 o'clock p.m.

It would be an officer's duty on arriving aboard his own or another vessel, to salute the quarter-deck by taking off his hat, even if there were nobody on the deck. All who were on the deck would return the salute also, by taking their hats off. An officer arriving on board his own vessel would always report to the captain of the vessel, as follows: "Captain, I report myself aboard, sir."

The captain would reply: "Aye, aye, sir."

Some very dark nights the Captain, in order to time the crew and officers of the *Valley City* in getting to their quarters, would spring the rattle for general quarters; and such a time there would be in getting out of our berths, and going to general quarters! The whole affair would be very amusing, and sometimes ridiculous.

The small boats attached to a man-of-war are the Captain's gig, dingy, cutters and launches. The man who guides or commands one of these small boats is known as the coxswain. A small boat is manned by seven to fifteen men, according to the size of the boat. The coxswain's command, if he wants to turn sharp to the left or port, is "Hold water port, give way strong starboard." If he wishes to turn sharp to the right or starboard, his command would be, "Hold water starboard, give way strong port." In rowing alongside of a vessel, when the boat had sufficient headway to carry it alongside, the coxswain commands the men to drop their oars. There are many other commands given by the coxswain, but it is unnecessary to name them in this place.

It is a very beautiful sight to see a boat rowed by fourteen trained men, all dressed similarly.

Saturday, December 31st, at 2 a.m., the *Valley City* got under weigh and proceeded up the Chowan River. We arrived in sight of Winton, when the *Valley City* returned down the river and anchored for the night. Sunday, January 1, 1865, at 4 o'clock p.m., we steamed down the river, and at 5½ o'clock p.m. we anchored off Edenton and went ashore. The weather is cold and windy.

Tuesday, January 3rd, 1865, the Valley City, at 10½ o'clock a.m., weighed anchor and proceeded to Plymouth, where she arrived at 1 p.m. At 8 p.m., left Plymouth and proceeded to off Edenton, where we arrived at 10 p.m.

Wednesday, January 4th, 1865, we left Edenton at 7 a.m., and arrived at Plymouth at 9½ a.m. Mr. Stevens is aboard. The weather is cold.

Saturday, January 7th.—During the week the *Valley City* has been cruising up Chowan River, Simon's Creek, and around Edenton Bay, watching for the Philadelphia, a blockade runner. Captain Brooks, Paymaster Sands and I, frequently went ashore at Edenton. The weather during the week has been mild, moist and rainy.

Sunday, January 8th, at 5 a.m., we proceeded from Chowan River to Edenton Bay, where we arrived at 7 a.m. Captain J. A. J. Brooks, Acting Master James G. Green, Paymaster Sands and I, went ashore and took dinner with Mr. Samuel B. At 6 p.m., we got under weigh and proceeded to the mouth of Chowan River. The weather is cold.

Monday, January 9th.—The weather is delightful. We lay during the day at the mouth of Chowan River. Tuesday, January 10th, at 5 a.m., the *Valley City* got under weigh and proceeded up to Poole's Landing, on the Chowan River. At 11:45 a.m., we discovered the Philadelphia. We immediately steamed toward her, and at 12:15 p.m., Mr. Milton Webster, executive officer, took a launch with a crew of men and boarded the Philadelphia, which was laying near Colerain, with a cargo of 257 bales of cotton, and tobacco. At 1 p.m. we got under weigh, with the Philadelphia in tow, and proceeded to Plymouth. At 5 p.m., we anchored at the mouth of Roanoke River. The weather is raining and blustering, accompanied with thunder and lightning.

Wednesday, January 11th, at 8 a.m., we weighed anchor and proceeded to Plymouth, where we arrived at 9½ a.m. At 1½ p.m., the *Valley City* got under weigh and proceeded to Edenton, where we arrived at 3:25th p.m. Captain Brooks, J. W. Sands and I, went ashore, and called on Mr. Samuel B. At 5:30 p.m. we got under weigh and proceeded to Plymouth, where we arrived at 8 p.m. The weather is cold but pleasant. At 9 p.m., we left Plymouth and proceeded up Chowan River.

Thursday, January 12th.—The *Valley City* came to anchor at 1 a.m., at Holly's Island. At 6 a.m. we got under weigh and proceeded up Chowan River. At 7:30 a.m. we came to anchor off "Camp Winfield." Mr. Milton Webster went ashore, and in company with Mr. Winslow, they travelled seven miles into the country, and returned safely at 1 p.m., with Mr. Winslow and his brother. In the meantime, Captain Brooks, Paymaster Sands and crew went ashore, and captured several bales of cotton. We arrived at Edenton at 7 p.m. Captain Brooks, Paymaster J. W. Sands, Mr. Cannon, and Messrs. Winslows, went ashore. The weather is delightful.

Friday, January 13th.—At 6:20 a.m. we got under weigh, and proceeded to Plymouth, where we arrived at 8:20 a.m. The weather is beautiful. I spent nearly all day ashore. At 7 p.m. we got under weigh, and proceeded toward Roanoke Island. Saturday, January 14, at 2 a.m., we anchored in Albemarle Sound, and at 8 a.m. we arrived at Roanoke Island. The weather is windy. Sunday, January 15, the *Valley City* got under weigh at 4 o'clock p.m., and proceeded toward Plymouth. Mr. O'Neill, acting master's mate, was very severely injured by a hawser to which the schooner was fastened in tow, slipping on a kevel. The weather is windy, and the Sounds are rough. Monday, January 16th, we arrived at Plymouth at 10 a.m.

Tuesday, January 17th.—We got under weigh at 11 a.m., and proceeded to Edenton, where we arrived at 12:30 p.m. Captain J. A. J. Brooks, Acting Master James G. Green, J. W. Sands and I went ashore and took tea at Mr. Samuel B—'s. We spent a very pleasant time. Mr. Skinner, D.D., was present. At 8 p.m. we got under weigh, and proceeded to Chowan River, and came to anchor at 9:25th p.m. for the night. The weather is delightful. Wednesday, January 18th, at 5 a.m. we got under weigh, and proceeded to Holly's Landing, where we anchored at 7 a.m.

Thursday, January 19th, at 9 a.m., we got under weigh, and proceeded to Edenton, where we arrived at 12 midnight. In the afternoon I attended the marriage of Acting Master James G. Green and Miss Cornelia B—, which took place at Mr. Samuel B—'s, the father of the bride. There were quite a number of the fleet's officers present. At 8 p.m., the *Valley City* proceeded towards Roanoke Island, with the bride and groom and the bride's two sisters and cousin aboard.

Friday, January 20th, at 1:30 a.m., we came to anchor, and at 8:30 a.m. we got under weigh, and arrived at Roanoke Island at 11:30 a.m.

Saturday, January 21st, 1865, I went ashore at Roanoke Island. The weather is rainy, foggy, and windy.

Monday, January 23rd, at 2 p.m., we got under weigh and proceeded to Plymouth, where we arrived in the evening. The night is dark and foggy.

Tuesday, January 24th, the *Valley City* arrived at Edenton, and landed the sisters and cousin of the bride, Acting Master James G. Green and his wife having proceeded from Roanoke Island north, on a short tour.

Saturday, January 28th, 1865.—At 6 a.m., the *Valley City* got under weigh and proceeded to Colerain, where we arrived at 10 a.m. The weather has been extraordinarily cold the last three days.

*Wednesday, February 1st.—*The weather has moderated and is pleasant. The *Valley City* is laying here for the purpose of protecting the troops ashore, commanded by Colonel Frankle, and for that purpose we shell the woods occasionally. The boat *Alison* ran against a snag here and was sunk, and is now being raised.

*Saturday, February 4th.—*At 5½ p.m., we got under weigh with boat *Alison* in tow, which had been previously raised so as to be buoyed up by two schooners, and arrived at Edenton Sunday.

February 5th, at 2 a.m., where we anchored the *Alison*, and at 11 a.m. we proceeded to Plymouth; but at the mouth of Middle River we were met by the tug *Belle*, from which we received orders to return to Edenton, to tow the *Alison* to Plymouth. We arrived at Edenton at 3 p.m., and at 7 p.m. the officers and two boats' crews went ashore. At 9 p.m. we took the *Alison* in tow, and arrived at the mouth of Roanoke River, where we anchored at 2 a.m., Monday, February 6. There is a rise in the Roanoke River, and its current is very swift, so that the *Valley City* could make but little headway up the river.

Thursday, February 9th, at 9¼ a.m., proceeded to Plymouth, where we arrived at 9¾ a.m.

Tuesday, February 21st, at 12 midnight., we weighed anchor and proceeded to Salmon's creek, where we arrived at 2:10 p.m. Here there were a number of contrabands and their effects taken on board. One of the contrabands stated she was 112 years of age, and had seen Washington in her early life; she is apparently very old. At 10 p.m., a boat, with a rebel soldier and two old men, with bacon, beef and fowls, were hailed, and the men and their effects were brought on board the *Valley City*.

Wednesday, February 22nd, at 6 a.m., the *Valley City* got under weigh and proceeded toward Plymouth. At 7 a.m., we came to an anchor off Walnut Point, and took on board more contrabands, and at 10 a.m. we proceeded to Plymouth, where we arrived at 11:20 a.m. At 3 p.m. we got under weigh, and arrived at Edenton at 5 p.m. I went ashore with Captain J. A. J. Brooks, and called on Mr. Samuel B—. The fleet at Plymouth fired a salute in commemoration of the birth of Washington.

Thursday, February 23rd, at 3 a.m., we got under weigh and proceeded to the mouth of Chowan River, and returned to Edenton, where we arrived at 8 a.m. Captain J. A. J. Brooks and I went ashore, and called on Messrs. Samuel B—, Henry B—, and Mr. M—. In the afternoon, we interred Matthew Sheridan, landsman, who had died of typhus fever. At 5 p.m. we returned to ship and got under weigh and proceeded down the *Albemarle* Sound to Laurel Point, where we arrived at 9 p.m., and anchored. The weather is pleasant.

Saturday, February 25th, at 5½ a.m., got under weigh and proceeded to the mouth of Little Alligator River, where we arrived and anchored at 9¼ a.m.

Sunday, February 26th, at 1½ p.m., the *Valley City* got under weigh and steamed toward Roanoke Island, in pursuit of a schooner which was supposed to be running the blockade; but upon boarding her, it was found she had permission to trade with the inhabitants in that vicinity. At 6 p.m., we came to an anchor at the mouth of Alligator River.

Monday, February 27th, at 6 a.m., the *Valley City* got under weigh and steamed up the Alligator River to Chincapin Ridge, where Captain J. A. J. Brooks, Acting Master's Mate O'Neill, and myself, with two crews of men, fourteen in number, went ashore and marched three miles into the country, through pines and cypresses. Along the road we put up a mark on a tree and fired at it; and although I was not an expert marksman, I put a ball nearest the mark. We finally came to a house occupied by a man and his wife and their children, who were very poor. The house was illy furnished, and had only one apartment. The appearance of it, inside or outside, was not very inviting. Captain J. A. J. Brooks asked the man whether he could provide dinner for the party. He demurred at first, but finally agreed to provide such a dinner as the viands in the house would permit of. All the party were very hungry, and were glad to have the opportunity of sitting down to any sort of a dinner. The woman went to work to cook a dinner. In the meantime, the officers, men, and host, employed themselves in shooting at a mark. During this time the host told us the war had been a benefit to him, in so far as it had made a temperance man of him. Before the war, he said, he had been an immoderate drinker of intoxicating liquors, but now he was temperate from necessity, as he could get nothing stronger than water to drink. Dinner was soon announced. It was set on a table about two feet square, without a tablecloth. Our dinner consisted of bacon, corn bread, and coffee made from corn. Only four could be seated at the same time around the table, consequently there were five successive tables served, occupying altogether about two hours in eating. We all enjoyed the dinner, as we were very hungry from travelling through the pines. After remunerating our host in a substantial way and thanking him for his hospitality, we returned to the vessel.

Tuesday, February 28th.—The *Valley City* got under weigh at 9 a.m., and arrived at Roanoke Island at 2:45 p.m. Wednesday, March 1, at 7 p.m., we weighed anchor and proceeded to Plymouth. At 10 p.m., we got aground near Croatan Sound.

Thursday, March 2nd, at 5½ o'clock a.m., we got under weigh and proceeded to Plymouth, where we arrived at 2 p.m. We brought with us as passengers Messrs. Douglass and Winslow, from Roanoke Island.

Saturday, March 4th, at 11 a.m., we proceeded to the mouth of Roanoke River, for the purpose of towing a coal schooner to Plymouth. We arrived at Plymouth at 3½ p.m. The weather has been very warm.

Wednesday, March 8th, at 8 p.m., we got under weigh and proceeded to Roanoke Island, where we arrived the following day at 6½ a.m. Mr. Harris, Second Assistant Engineer, and I, went ashore.

Friday, March 10th, at 9½ a.m., we got under weigh, and at 1 p.m. anchored in Albemarle Sound. As the *Valley City* was steaming toward Plymouth, suddenly and unexpectedly a heavy squall came up, and tossed the *Valley City* about so much that we were fearful she might be capsized. The guns were not made fast at the time. The officers had just sat down to dinner as the *Valley City* commenced rolling and pitching tremendously. First we endeavoured to save the contents of the dinner table; finally this effort was abandoned in order to save ourselves. We were tossed about the ward-room in an uncomfortable manner. The contents of the dinner table went to the floor and were lost, and to mend matters the *Valley City* got into the "trough of the sea." The howitzers and ammunition above our heads on the poop deck, were being tossed from side to side, and so were also the large guns on the gun deck. The line officers and crew were soon engaged in getting the *Valley City* out of the "trough of the sea," and securing her guns by making them fast. The gale continued about a half hour, after which the *Valley City* steamed quietly to Plymouth.

Saturday, March 11th, at 11:20 a.m., we anchored off Edenton, and at 4:35 p.m., proceeded to Plymouth, where we arrived at 7:15 p.m.

Wednesday, March 15th, the *Valley City* got under weigh and proceeded to the blockade above Plymouth.

Monday, March 20th, the *Valley City* got under weigh and proceeded to the mouth of the Cashie River, where we arrived at 2 p.m.

Wednesday, March 22nd, the *Valley City* got under weigh and proceeded to Plymouth, where we arrived at 3½ p.m.

At 4½ p.m., we got under weigh and proceeded to Edenton, where we arrived at 6½ p.m. Captain J. A. J. Brooks, Paymaster J. W. Sands, Major Willis, Mr. Tiffing and myself, went ashore.

Friday, March 24th, at 5 p.m., we got under weigh and proceeded to Plymouth, where we arrived at 7 p.m. The weather is beautiful. Saturday, March 25th, at 1½ p.m., Commander Macomb came aboard, and the *Valley City* proceeded toward Newbern. At 8½ p.m., we anchored in Croatan Sound.

Sunday, March 26th, at 5½ a.m., we got under weigh, and at 7½ a.m. we came to anchor. At 10¼ a.m. we got under weigh and proceeded to Newbern, where we arrived the following day at 1 a.m.

Friday, March 31st, at 3 o'clock, a.m., we left Newbern, with Commander Macomb still aboard, and arrived at Roanoke Island at 5¾ p.m. At 7 p.m. we got under weigh, and proceeded as far as Croatan Sound, where we got aground, and stuck fast till the following day, when at 12½ a.m. we got afloat, and anchored till 5 a.m., when we proceeded to Plymouth, where we arrived at 2 p.m. Commander Macomb went on board his own ship, the *Shamrock*. At 4½ p.m. we got under weigh, and proceeded by way of Albemarle Sound and Chowan River to Winton, and then up Meherrin River to Murfreesborough, N.C., in company with the U.S. Steamers *Shamrock, Wyalusing*, and Hunchback. We dragged the Meherrin River for torpedoes from Winton to Murfreesborough, but found none, arriving at Murfreesborough on Monday, April 3, at 6:35 p.m.

Murfreesborough is a small, beautifully-located town, on a high plateau of ground on the right bank of the Meherrin River, surrounded by woods. There were two female seminaries in the place, one a Baptist, the other a Methodist. The people were intelligent, but very much interested in the success of the Confederacy. This place was opened up by the fleet for the purpose of being a depot of supply for Sherman's army, and was intended to be the next point of landing after Sherman left Raleigh. In Murfreesborough there were about one thousand rebels, who gave us great annoyance till they were finally captured by the 3rd New York cavalry.

On the following Tuesday, April 4th, Acting Ensign Milton Webster and myself went ashore for the purpose of ascertaining the whereabouts of Paymaster J. W. Sands, who had previously gone ashore. At a point midway between the cliff of the river and the town, we met a coloured man who told us we had better be careful, as there were rebel cavalry in the town. We then went away from the town in a line parallel with the river, across a ravine which was at right angles with the river. Just as we had crossed the ravine, we saw the rebel cavalry coming down on the opposite side. We took to our heels and ran under fire till we got to the woods, and thence to the fleet. When we arrived aboard the *Valley City*, we found that Paymaster Sands had returned on board, and had taken about the same route ashore as we had.

Wednesday, April 5th, the marines were put in line and marched into the town under cover of the fleet; but as they marched in the rebels marched out. Acting Ensign J. B. Fairchilds was very seriously wounded by an accidental discharge of his own pistol before starting.

Thursday, April 6th, several officers and men of the fleet were ashore, but did not go into the town. In the afternoon many of our men approached near the city, where the rebel cavalry could be seen plainly. Paymaster J. W. Sands and I had walked about one-half the distance from the river towards the town, when we saw the rebel cavalry. We then returned nearer the river, to a cabin in which two very old coloured people lived, in the rear of a large log on which Captain J. A. J. Brooks was standing, we both went into the cabin. After a few minutes' stay there in conversation with the coloured people, I happened to look out of the window and saw the officers and men of the fleet running. I immediately said to Paymaster Sands, "The rebels are coming!" Then we ran out of the cabin under fire down toward the fleet. The bullets fell all around me as I was running, and just as I came to a path which led down the cliff, on which a lot of scrub oak was growing, the fleet opened fire, and the branches of the trees over my head were cut by the flying shells. I immediately fell out of range *of* the *shells*, and took an unfrequented path which led to the mouth of the ravine. I soon arrived at the mouth of the ravine, near by the river. Meantime the fleet was keeping up a rapid fire. The remainder of the officers and men came down, but soon learned our supposed enemy was the 3rd New York cavalry, who also thought we were Confederates. This cavalry force had made a raid from Weldon, and had approached the town from the opposite side from where the fleet was laying, and in so doing captured the rebel cavalry in the town of Murfreesborough. There was fortunately nobody injured. The horses of the cavalry were covered with foam and very much heated—so much so that the saddles were taken from their backs, and they were led around for an hour before they cooled off.

The same afternoon, after the third New York cavalry had arrived, many of the officers of the fleet, feeling they might visit the town with impunity, did so. Captain J. A. J. Brooks, Lieutenant Joseph P. Fyffe of the Hunchback, James M. Battin, chief engineer of the *Valley City*, Paymaster J. W. Sands and myself, by invitation, took tea with a Mr. C—of the place.

The next morning, Thursday, April 6, the third New York cavalry marched through the main street and left the town. All the windows of the houses on the main street were closed, and none of their occupants were to be seen. This was done in contempt for the Federal troops. After our cavalry had departed, the officers and the marines returned to the fleet, and at 4:15 p.m. got under weigh, and arrived off Winton at 10 p.m., where the fleet remained for some time.

Wednesday, April 10th, at 12 midnight., the *Valley City* got under weigh and proceeded by way of Edenton to Plymouth, where we arrived at 2:15 a.m. the following day. At 3:05 a.m. we got under weigh and returned to Winton, where we arrived at 12 midnight. At this point and time we first heard, through the New York *Herald*, that the Confederate troops under General Lee had been driven from Petersburg by the Federal troops under General U.S. Grant. There was great rejoicing aboard the fleet. The U.S. steamers *Shamrock*, *Wyalusing* and Hunchback, fired a salute in celebration of that event. At 3½ p.m. the U.S. steamers *Valley City* and *Whitehead* proceeded to Murfreesborough, where we arrived at 6½ p.m.

Friday, April 14th, at 7:50 a.m., the *Valley City* and *Whitehead* got under weigh, and proceeded down to Winton, where we met the Wilderness, with Commander Wm. H. Macomb and Lieutenant Commander Earl English aboard, when we received the news that the Confederate forces under General Lee had surrendered to General Grant.

The U.S. steamers *Valley City* and *Whitehead* were ordered to proceed to Murfreesborough and deliver the news to the citizens at that place; and now, after having read a copy of the *New York Herald*, they were thoroughly convinced that the war was over.

Saturday, April 15th, at 11:45 a.m., the U.S. steamers *Valley City* and *Whitehead* got under weigh and proceeded to Winton, where we arrived at 7:55 p.m.

Tuesday, April 18th, we first received news of President Lincoln's assassination, which event cast a gloom over the entire nation. At 12:45 p.m., the U.S. steamers *Valley City* and *Whitehead* got under weigh and proceeded up the Chowan River to Blackwater River, up which we steamed to Franklin, Virginia, where we arrived at 8 a.m. the following day. We visited the people ashore at different times during our stay at that place.

Thursday, April 20th, at 8½ a.m., the *Valley City* and *Whitehead* got under weigh, and proceeded down the Blackwater River to Chowan River, down which we steamed to its mouth, where we anchored.

There are a great many fish in the Chowan River, and the *Valley City* has often caught shad and herring by the barrel, in a large seine which the inhabitants of that vicinity use for the purpose.

Saturday, April 22nd, at 4:25 a.m., the U.S. steamers *Valley City* and *Whitehead* got under weigh, and at 8:30 a.m. arrived at Plymouth, where we anchored. At 3:20 p.m., the *Valley City* and *Whitehead* got under weigh, and arrived at Edenton at 5:30 p.m., and at 11 p.m. the *Valley City* and *Whitehead* got under weigh and steamed toward Hertford, N.C., where we arrived on Sunday, April 23rd, at 7½ a.m. At 10 a.m. the officers of the two vessels in full uniform went to an Episcopal service held in a church in Hertford. The members of the congregation were sparsely scattered on seats throughout the church. Upon the officers entering and occupying two pews on the left hand side of the church, that portion of the congregation occupying the same range of seats as ourselves very abruptly and hurriedly sought seats on the other side. After listening to a sermon which was nervously delivered, we quietly and orderly returned aboard our respective vessels.

Hertford is a small town on a body of water extending from Albemarle Sound, called Perquimans. The people were usually kind and courteous, after they discovered that our disposition was to be friendly toward them. There were people living there who were in sympathy with the Federal government, and to whose hospitality we were kindly invited and welcomed. One day during our stay at Hertford, Paymaster J. W. Sands and myself procured a buggy and horse, and drove to Edenton, a distance of twenty miles, and returned to Hertford in the evening. The trip was not considered a very safe one, on account of the number of bushwhackers there had been in that vicinity.

Monday, May 1st, at 8½ a.m., the *Valley City* got under weigh, and arrived at Edenton at 2:10 p.m.; and at 5 p.m. left Edenton and arrived at Plymouth at 7 p.m.

Tuesday, May 9, the *Valley City* got under weigh for the purpose of clearing the Roanoke River of torpedoes. The U.S. steamer *Iosco*, commanded by Lieutenant Commander James S. Thornton, accompanied us.

Saturday, May 13th, the *Valley City* and *Iosco* arrived at Hamilton, N.C. Captain Thornton, Third Assistant Engineer Amos Harris, Ensign Hull, and myself went ashore and spent the afternoon. In the morning before arriving at Hamilton, Lieutenant-Commander James S. Thornton of the *Iosco* went ashore, and visited Rainbow Bluff. Captain Thornton made the remark that the place would have been very difficult to capture with any naval force, so strongly was it fortified.

Lieutenant-Commander James S. Thornton was executive officer aboard the U.S. steamer *Kearsarge* at the time this vessel sunk the rebel blockade runner Alabama, in which the transaction was so quick and complete. Captain Thornton stated that at 11 o'clock a.m., of a Sunday, when he received the report of there being a ship in sight, he was seated in a chair, with his feet resting on the wardroom table, reading the Bible. The rattle for general quarters was rung, and the *Kearsarge* got under weigh, and proceeded toward the Alabama, sunk her, and by 2 o'clock of the same afternoon the *Kearsarge* arrived at Cherbourg, France. Comments by the citizens of that place were made on the cleanliness of the *Kearsarge* after sinking so formidable a vessel as the Alabama.

Monday, May 15th, at 1 p.m., the *Valley City* arrived at Palmyra, N.C. I visited the town. It is a place of about a half-a-dozen houses, about a mile from the right bank of the Roanoke River. At this place Captain J. A. J. Brooks joined the *Valley City* with the *Cotton Plant* and *Fisher*, two steamers which the Confederates had captured from the Federals at Plymouth at the time the *Southfield* was sunk by the rebel ram *Albemarle*. There were aboard these boats fifty bales of cotton. In the evening, pilot John A. Wilson ran the *Valley City* hard and fast aground, so that it took the greater part of the night to get her afloat.

Thursday, May 16th, the *Valley City* steamed up to Ergot's Landing, and took aboard thirty-nine bales of cotton. Thursday, May 18th, the *Valley City* got under weigh and proceeded down the Roanoke River and came to anchor five miles above Hamilton.

Saturday, May 20th, at 9 a.m., the *Valley City* got under weigh, and proceeded to Hamilton, where we came to an anchor.

Tuesday, May 23, in the morning Captain J. A. J. Brooks, Paymaster J. W. Sands and myself went hunting for squir rels. Paymaster Sands separated from us early in the morning. The Captain and I soon came to a mulberry tree, on which he shot a squirrel which was after mulberries; another came and was shot, and before night we shot a dozen. In the evening, upon returning to the vessel, we met Paymaster Sands, who was also returning to the vessel. He had been travelling all day in the woods, but did not shoot a squirrel. We all proceeded to the *Valley City*, and had the squirrels cooked for supper, of which we ate heartily, for we were very hungry. This was the last supper I ate aboard the *Valley City*.

Wednesday, May 24, at 5:30 o'clock, I was relieved by Acting Assistant Surgeon L. W. Loring, and ordered North on a two months leave of absence; and now I am to say farewell to the officers and crew of the *Valley City*, with whom I have shared their dangers, their sorrows and their joys, and the old ship I am also to leave, which has buoyed us so safely over the short and rugged waves of the waters of North Carolina, amidst the torpedoes, the sharpshooters, and the artillery of the enemy. This is certainly an occasion of joy, yet mingled with sadness.

Farewell is a word that has been, a word that must be, a sound which makes us linger—yet we must say, farewell.

HOMEWARD BOUND

I went aboard the *Eolus*, which proceeded up the Roanoke River, and at 4:30 p.m. we met the *Cotton Plant*, with Commander W. H. Macomb aboard, eight miles below Halifax. The *Eolus*, with the *Cotton Plant*, returned to Edward's Ferry, where we arrived at 7 p.m. I went ashore. This place, which is a large plantation, and was owned by Mr. Wm. Smith, who owns, or did own, quite a number of slaves, who worked the plantation. At this time the slaves were cultivating corn. The male slaves, with hoes to hoe the corn, followed after the female slaves, who drove the horses and directed the cultivators or ploughs. The rebel ram *Albemarle* was constructed at Edward's Ferry, and there was another ram or iron-clad in process of construction at this place; but it was destroyed by the rebels at the close of the war. I saw the landing where these rams were constructed; the chips from them could be seen lying all around.

Thursday, May 25th.—We left Edward's Ferry at 10 a.m., and at 8 p.m. the *Eolus* came to an anchor near Poplar Point, where we visited the graves of those who had been killed in the late action at this place.

Friday, May 26th.—The *Eolus*, with Commander W. H. Macomb on board, got under weigh and steamed to Plymouth, where we arrived at 12 midnight. Commander W. H. Macomb went aboard his own vessel, the *Shamrock*. At 8 p.m. the *Eolus* got under weigh and steamed towards Roanoke Island, and came to an anchor at 12 p.m. in Albemarle Sound.

Saturday, May 27th, at 4½ a.m., the *Eolus* got under weigh and proceeded to Roanoke Island, where we arrived at 7:15 a.m. At 2½ p.m. I took passage in the boat Washington Irving, which got under weigh and steamed till 9½ p.m., when I changed into the boat *Arrow*, which steamed two miles up the Dismal Swamp canal, and passed by the wreck of the *Fawn*, which had been previously captured, sunk and burned by the rebels, and there came to an anchor. During the night I slept on a bench, with my boot for a pillow.

Sunday, May 28th, the boat *Arrow* left Coinjock at 5 a.m., and arrived at Norfolk, Va., at 1 p.m. I took dinner at the National House in that place. At 2½ p.m. I took passage from Norfolk in the *Louisiana*, and arrived at Fortress Monroe at 3½ p.m. We passed by the wreck of the rebel iron-clad *Merrimac.* At 5 p.m. the *Louisiana* got under weigh for Baltimore, where she arrived

Monday, May 29th, at 6 o'clock a.m.; I went by way of Philadelphia home, where I arrived about noon of May 30, 1865.

The atmosphere never seemed to me more salubrious than at this time; the grass never appeared greener, the flowers never seemed to exhale more fragrance, and the people never seemed kinder. It seemed a perfect Paradise compared with the swamps of North Carolina.

During the time of my "leave of absence," I met with the following men of note, all of whom are now dead: Hon. Thaddeus Stevens I met in the reading-room of the United States Hotel at Harrisburg, Pa., seated on a chair with his feet resting on a table, reading the newspapers, a number of files of which he had lying all around him. He would first glance at one file and then at another, till he had examined all. I have heard of two anecdotes told about him. One was, whilst meeting an enemy face to face on the street in Lancaster, Pa., his enemy said to Mr. Stevens, "I never turn out of the road of a fool." The latter said sharply, "I do," and passed around the former. The other incident occurred whilst Mr. Stevens was very ill in Washington, D.C. A friend visited him and complimented him on his appearance. Mr. Stevens very jocularly replied that it was not his appearance that interested him (Mr. Stevens) so much as his disappearance. I have since visited his grave in Lancaster, Pa., which has the following inscription upon the tombstone:

Thaddeus Stevens

Born at Danville, Caledonia County, Vermont

April 4, 1792

Died at Washington, D.C.

August 11, 1868

STEVENS

I repose in this quiet and secluded spot,
Not from any preference for solitude,
But finding other cemeteries limited as
to race by charter rules,
I have chosen this, that I might illustrate in my death
the principle which I advocated through a long life,
Equality of man before his Creator

1792-1868

I also met in Lancaster, Pa., about the same time, ex-President James Buchanan. But in the month of June, 1862, I had the curiosity to call on that gentleman at his home near Lancaster, called Wheatland. I found an affable, friendly, heavy-set and gray-haired old gentleman, seated in a chair in his library. After entering into conversation with him upon general topics, he touched upon his early life, his struggles as a young man in the profession of law, his nomination and election to the Presidency of the United States, and also upon his occupancy of that office. There was anticipation at that time of Richmond being captured on or before the coming Fourth of July. I asked Mr. Buchanan if he thought Richmond would be captured by that time. He replied that he did not, but he hoped that the war for the preservation of the Union would be successfully terminated by the following July a year. I then asked him if he thought Napoleon would give his aid to the Confederacy, as it was rumoured at that time that he would do so. He answered that Napoleon was a man who kept his own counsel. During my stay there, there was a gentleman called upon him for the purpose of soliciting aid in defraying the expenses of celebrating the coming Fourth of July at Lancaster, Pa. He contributed liberally, and told the solicitor if the amount he had already given him was not sufficient, to call again, and he would contribute more.

I have since visited his grave at Lancaster, Pa., which has the following inscription upon the tombstone:

Here rest the remains of
James Buchanan
Fifteenth President of the United States
Born in Franklin County, Pa.
April 23rd, 1781
Died at Wheatland
January 1, 1868

(Second side.) 1781–1868

(Third side.) BUCHANAN

I also called on Dr. Samuel Jackson, who, during a long and extended practice in his profession, had been at one time Henry Clay's physician. I attended a course of his lectures at the Medical Department of the University of Pennsylvania. He had lost the use of his lower extremities, and was seated in a chair, at his home in Philadelphia, Pa. He stated he had from early life to the present been a hard student; and as he was about to pass through the portal of this life into another, he expected still to be a student there. He stated that it had at different times of his life been a matter of serious consideration as to how much inflammable matter in a given time the sun used in warming the space included in the solar system. He said he expected to be able to make this calculation in another life.

I also met with General James L. Kiernan, in New York city. I was called to attend him whilst visiting in that city, in an attack of congestive chills, which he had contracted whilst on duty in the State of *Louisiana*. He had stumped several of the northern States for President Lincoln's second election, and had been appointed United States Consul to China after that election. He filled this office till the close of President Johnson's administration. He was a man about forty-five years of age, an excellent conversationalist, a good companion, and a fine orator.

On September 23, 1865, I was ordered to Cairo, Ill., for duty aboard the U.S. monitors *Oneota* and *Catawba*, as a relief to Acting Assistant Surgeon Geo. C. Osgood. I reported to Commodore J. W. Livingston for duty October 6, 1865, having arrived in Cairo on the previous evening. I stopped at the St. Charles Hotel all night. The weather was very hot and dry, the river was low, and for a distance along shore an unhealthy green foam had gathered along the edge of the river. Congestive chills were quite prevalent there that fall.

Cairo is a large and thriving town, situated at the extreme southern point of the state of Illinois. Many of the houses then were built on stilts or posts. The sidewalks were also resting on stilts or posts, so that in crossing a street a person would have to walk down a pair of stairs, then across the street, and mount another pair of stairs. During the time of a rise in the Mississippi or Ohio River, the place was flooded, and then the citizens would use boats for the purpose of navigating from place to place. The town was somewhat protected from overflows by levees.

The monitors were very nicely finished and furnished inside. The deck was about six inches above water. There were four monitors anchored in line in the middle of the Ohio River off Cairo. The names of them were as follows: *Oneota*, *Catawba*, *Manyyunk* and *Tippecanoe*. The officers of all these vessels messed aboard the U.S. monitor *Oneota*. Acting Lieutenant Commander Wells was the captain of the *Oneota*. He was afterwards relieved by Acting Master H. E. Bartlett. Thomas Cook was her chief engineer, and

Don Carlos Hasseltino was chief engineer of the monitor *Catawba*. One of the officers of the *Oneota* was a persistent story-teller, and the only way to get him to stop telling his story was to suggest to him to make a chalk mark and finish the remainder of it the following day. One day, early in the morning, he and I went ashore in Kentucky, hunting; and hunted all day without any dinner. I got very tired and left him, and returned to the boat, which was made fast ashore opposite to the junction of the Mississippi and Ohio rivers, where I lay down on a brush-heap and fell asleep; but when my companion started to row to the *Oneota*, the rattling of the oars awakened me, otherwise I would have been left. One time, during a freshet in the Ohio River, I think in January, I had occasion to go to one of the monitors anchored in the rear of the *Oneota*. After arriving on that monitor, in our attempt to return, I found that the boat could make no headway against the current. We struck over along the Kentucky bank of the river, and did what the sailor calls "cheating the current;" that is, we rowed up along the bank of the river. After rowing above the *Oneota*, we crossed the bows of the *Oneota* and threw out the end of a painter, which was instantly tied around the stanchion of the *Oneota*. The painter broke, and down the river the boat was carried by the current; but somebody aboard the *Oneota* threw the end of a rope overboard, which we caught, and we were pulled back aboard. Another time during the freshet, Mr. Thomas Cook and I went ashore, and were nearly carried by the swift current between two packet boats, but we fortunately saved ourselves.

A pilot wishing to cross with a packet-boat before or in front of the *Oneota*'s bows, from a landing on the Cairo side of the river to the Kentucky side, ran the boat into the *Oneota*, and the packet was sunk. The packet-boat was laden with passengers, who were all saved.

Don Carlos Hasseltino was chief engineer of the U.S. monitor *Catawba*, but spent most of his time on board the U.S. monitor *Oneota*, and was one of the mess-mates of that vessel. I associated with him constantly from October 6, 1865, to January 16th, 1866. He was a jolly, kind, sympathetic, and intelligent associate. In height he was about six feet, and had a large, wiry frame. His hair and eyes were black; he wore a black moustache. He never gave offence to any one, but would not suffer himself to be insulted. He carried two Derringers in leather pockets buttoned to his pantaloons above the hips. He was very polite and chivalrous; woe to the person that gave offense or offered insult. I insert here a sketch of his life.

FROM THE *CINCINNATI ENQUIRER* OF 1880
A LIFE OF ADVENTURE.
GENERAL DON CARLOS HASSELTINO'S STORY
OF HIS STARTLING CAREER
REBEL SPY AND UNION OFFICER
HIS ADVENTURE IN THE ARMY
IN PERU AS A CUBAN REFUGEE

General Don Carlos Hasseltino was met by an *Enquirer* reporter on a Wabash train the other day. His life has been one of adventure. Previous to the war he graduated at Oxford, in Butler county, in the same class with the gallant Joe Battle, who, with his brother, fell beside their father at Shiloh, while fighting under the flag of the Lost Cause. After graduating he went to Hamilton and read law with Judge Clark, who acquired some notoriety at Hamilton by his advocacy of the right of secession in 18th60-61. When the war begun, Hasseltino determined to risk his fortunes with the Confederacy. He started South under the pretext of escorting to her husband in Tennessee

Mrs. Dallie, the wife of Adjutant Joe Battle, of the Sixth Tennessee. They passed south from Louisville on the last train which left that city before the war, and arrived at Nashville. From there, young Hasseltino went to Montgomery, Ala., then the Confederate capital, where he was appointed Major, and a little later Lieutenant-Colonel; and was ordered to Pensacola, Fla. When that place fell into the hands of the National troops, he was captured; but within a day or two he made his escape. His next point of duty was at Fort McHenry, from whence he went to Louisville and bought for the Confederate troops a quantity of supplies, and succeeded in getting them safely within the Confederate lines. When General Grant was advancing upon Fort Donaldson, he went out as a spy, and spent most of three days with the Federals. Being recognized, he was ordered to be shot at nine o'clock in the evening, but in the rain and darkness made his escape, and reached the fort at daylight the next morning, drenched and almost frozen. Upon his report being heard, it was decided to evacuate the fort with most of the forces. From Island No. 10 he fell back to Memphis; and, believing that nothing would stay the victorious march of the Union arms, sent in his resignation, which was accepted.

Securing a Pass North

When the Federals occupied Memphis he remained here, trusting to nerve and luck to get away. To his horror he learned the next day that Colonel Alexander, of the Forty-eighth Indiana, with whom he was at college, was made Provost Marshal of the post, and that no one could leave the city except on a pass issued by him. He had some knowledge of French, and had grown quite a beard since leaving school, and he determined to take the risk. Walking into the Colonel's room, with many shrugs and gesticulations he asked for a *'Permissio San Louie,'* and urged it with such vehemence that the Colonel finally said to his assistant, 'Give the d—d Frenchman a pass to St. Louis.' While going up the river he was in constant dread of recognition, but fortunately did not meet a soul whom he knew. Hardly had he landed when he met a former school-mate and intimate friend from Hamilton, who was then Assistant Engineer in the Navy. His friend knew that he had gone south, and accused him of being in St. Louis as a spy. This he denied, and then told him all the details of his adventures, and finally appealed to his friend for advice as to what he should do or where he should go, for he began to feel unsafe there. His friend advised him not to return to Hamilton, where he would be in certain danger; and finally suggested that he apply for an appointment as an assistant engineer in the navy. 'Why, I don't know a steam-engine from a horse-power,' was his answer. But his friend proposed to help him out, and provided him with a lot of books, which would teach him all the theory; and at them he went; and in six weeks he went before the Examining Board and passed as a first assistant engineer, and was ordered to duty on the gunboat *Essex*, the flag-ship of Commodore Porter, who was in command of the Mississippi river flotilla. This was jumping out of the frying-pan into the fire. He knew nothing practically of the engine, thinking then, as he told his friend, that 'the pumping engine must be for the purpose of moving the vessel sidewise.' But luck was on his side. While lying in port, or before going to duty, he got a few talks with Commodore Porter, and succeeded in getting to the rank of Chief Engineer in the navy, and assigned to duty on the staff of the Commodore. If those who read this will take the trouble to read the report of the Secretary of the Navy to Congress in 1864, they will find that that official transmitted to Congress that part of Commodore Porter's report which embraces a report of Chief Engineer Hasseltino on the construction of iron-clad gunboats, and recommended the adoption of the report.

Inspecting Government Iron-Clads

After the close of the ill-fated Red River campaign, Hasseltino was ordered to St. Louis to inspect and superintend the construction of the iron-clads which were being built by McCord & Co. But just before leaving his vessel he had a quarrel with a fellow-officer, whom he challenged; but when the challenge was declined he opened on the other party with a battery of Derringers, fortunately missing the object of his aim.

In 1865, he went to some European port and brought a blockade runner, the name of which I have forgotten. In the early part of 1866, he was mustered out of service and went to New Orleans, intending to go into business. In the July riots he was shot through the shoulder; and, thinking the climate unhealthy, went to St. Louis. Here he fell in with a representative of the government of Chile, and went to South America.

In an attack on Callao—for Peru and Chile were at war—he fell into the hands of the Peruvians, and with his usual luck was sentenced to be shot. By bribing the guards, he succeeded in escaping and making his way on board of an English vessel, and was landed at Panama. Crossing the Isthmus to Aspinwall, he found a vessel ready to leave for New Orleans; and, though without money, managed to secure a passage to that place.

Without money he was naturally open for any adventure, and a representative of the Cuban rebellion was the first to offer him a chance. He sailed directly to Nuevitas, and before he had been in that port a week had fallen in love with a young Cuban widow, who, though childless, was possessed of an immense plantation. After the briefest possible courtship, they were married in the latter part of 1867 or early in 1868; within three months of the wedding she died from yellow fever; and before the end of the year her estate, which he had inherited, was confiscated, and he barely escaped with his life, landing in Florida in an open boat and in a half-starved condition, without friends or money. He managed to reach Indianapolis in July, 1869, when a naval acquaintance and friend, James Noble, gave him an outfit of clothes and money sufficient to take him to Chicago. Here he determined to locate, and went to work to find business. He got an agency for the sale of coal, and soon had quite a start in the coal business. When the Chicago fire broke out, on that dreadful Sunday night, he was out on the lake boating with a party of friends. When he got back, the conflagration had swept his little coal pile, his office and sleeping room, and he was again left in the world without a change of clothes, and with less than five dollars in money. The third day of the fire he was found by Otto Hasselman, of the *Indianapolis Journal*, who was on the ground with a corps of reporters; and by him sent to Indianapolis, where he was again furnished with an outfit and a ticket to St. Louis. Shortly after reaching that place he entered the service of the wholesale house of R. L. Billingsley & Co., and remained with them until a year ago, when he purchased a farm in Illinois.

January 16th, 1866, I received a two month's "leave of absence," at the expiration of which I received the following discharge:

United States of America
Navy Department
The war for the preservation of the Union having, under the beneficent guidance of Almighty God, been brought to a successful termination, a reduction of the naval force becomes necessary.

Having served with fidelity in the United States Navy from the 22nd day of March, 1864, to the present date, you are hereby honourably discharged with the thanks of the Department.

Given under my hand and seal, at the city of Washington, this 23rd day of March, one thousand eight hundred and sixty-six.

Gideon Welles
Secretary of the Navy
Acting Assistant Surgeon, John M. Batten
U.S. Navy
Guthrieville, Pa.

LEONAUR

ALSO FROM LEONAUR
AVAILABLE IN SOFTCOVER OR HARDCOVER WITH DUST JACKET

A HISTORY OF THE FRENCH & INDIAN WAR *by Arthur G. Bradley*—The Seven Years War as it was fought in the New World has always fascinated students of military history—here is the story of that confrontation.

WASHINGTON'S EARLY CAMPAIGNS *by James Hadden*—The French Post Expedition, Great Meadows and Braddock's Defeat—including Braddock's Orderly Books.

BOUQUET & THE OHIO INDIAN WAR *by Cyrus Cort & William Smith*—Two Accounts of the Campaigns of 1763-1764: Bouquet's Campaigns by Cyrus Cort & The History of Bouquet's Expeditions by William Smith.

NARRATIVES OF THE FRENCH & INDIAN WAR: 2 *by David Holden, Samuel Jenks, Lemuel Lyon, Mary Cochrane Rogers & Henry T. Blake*—Contains The Diary of Sergeant David Holden, Captain Samuel Jenks' Journal, The Journal of Lemuel Lyon, Journal of a French Officer at the Siege of Quebec, A Battle Fought on Snowshoes & The Battle of Lake George.

NARRATIVES OF THE FRENCH & INDIAN WAR *by Brown, Eastburn, Hawks & Putnam*—Ranger Brown's Narrative, The Adventures of Robert Eastburn, The Journal of Rufus Putnam—Provincial Infantry & Orderly Book and Journal of Major John Hawks on the Ticonderoga-Crown Point Campaign.

THE 7TH (QUEEN'S OWN) HUSSARS: Volume 1: 1688-1792 *by C. R. B. Barrett*—As Dragoons During the Flanders Campaign, War of the Austrian Succession and the Seven Years War.

INDIA'S FREE LANCES *by H. G. Keene*—European Mercenary Commanders in Hindustan 1770-1820.

THE BENGAL EUROPEAN REGIMENT *by P. R. Innes*—An Elite Regiment of the Honourable East India Company 1756-1858.

MUSKET & TOMAHAWK *by Francis Parkman*—A Military History of the French & Indian War, 1753-1760.

THE BLACK WATCH AT TICONDEROGA *by Frederick B. Richards*—Campaigns in the French & Indian War.

QUEEN'S RANGERS *by Frederick B. Richards*—John Simcoe and his Rangers During the Revolutionary War for America.

LEONAUR

ALSO FROM LEONAUR
AVAILABLE IN SOFTCOVER OR HARDCOVER WITH DUST JACKET

LEONAUR

ALSO FROM LEONAUR
AVAILABLE IN SOFTCOVER OR HARDCOVER WITH DUST JACKET

OFFICERS & GENTLEMEN *by Peter Hawker & William Graham*—Two Accounts of British Officers During the Peninsula War: Officer of Light Dragoons by Peter Hawker & Campaign in Portugal and Spain by William Graham .

THE WALCHEREN EXPEDITION *by Anonymous*—The Experiences of a British Officer of the 81st Regt. During the Campaign in the Low Countries of 1809.

LADIES OF WATERLOO *by Charlotte A. Eaton, Magdalene de Lancey & Juana Smith*—The Experiences of Three Women During the Campaign of 1815: Waterloo Days by Charlotte A. Eaton, A Week at Waterloo by Magdalene de Lancey & Juana's Story by Juana Smith.

JOURNAL OF AN OFFICER IN THE KING'S GERMAN LEGION *by John Frederick Hering*—Recollections of Campaigning During the Napoleonic Wars.

JOURNAL OF AN ARMY SURGEON IN THE PENINSULAR WAR *by Charles Boutflower*—The Recollections of a British Army Medical Man on Campaign During the Napoleonic Wars.

ON CAMPAIGN WITH MOORE AND WELLINGTON *by Anthony Hamilton*—The Experiences of a Soldier of the 43rd Regiment During the Peninsular War.

THE ROAD TO AUSTERLITZ *by R. G. Burton*—Napoleon's Campaign of 1805.

SOLDIERS OF NAPOLEON *by A. J. Doisy De Villargennes & Arthur Chuquet*—The Experiences of the Men of the French First Empire: Under the Eagles by A. J. Doisy De Villargennes & Voices of 1812 by Arthur Chuquet .

INVASION OF FRANCE, 1814 *by F. W. O. Maycock*—The Final Battles of the Napoleonic First Empire.

LEIPZIG—A CONFLICT OF TITANS *by Frederic Shoberl*—A Personal Experience of the 'Battle of the Nations' During the Napoleonic Wars, October 14th-19th, 1813.

SLASHERS *by Charles Cadell*—The Campaigns of the 28th Regiment of Foot During the Napoleonic Wars by a Serving Officer.

BATTLE IMPERIAL *by Charles William Vane*—The Campaigns in Germany & France for the Defeat of Napoleon 1813-1814.

SWIFT & BOLD *by Gibbes Rigaud*—The 60th Rifles During the Peninsula War.

LEONAUR

ALSO FROM LEONAUR
AVAILABLE IN SOFTCOVER OR HARDCOVER WITH DUST JACKET

CAPTAIN COIGNET *by Jean-Roch Coignet*—A Soldier of Napoleon's Imperial Guard from the Italian Campaign to Russia and Waterloo.

HUSSAR ROCCA *by Albert Jean Michel de Rocca*—A French cavalry officer's experiences of the Napoleonic Wars and his views on the Peninsular Campaigns against the Spanish, British And Guerilla Armies.

MARINES TO 95TH (RIFLES) *by Thomas Fernyhough*—The military experiences of Robert Fernyhough during the Napoleonic Wars.

LIGHT BOB *by Robert Blakeney*—The experiences of a young officer in H.M 28th & 36th regiments of the British Infantry during the Peninsular Campaign of the Napoleonic Wars 1804 - 1814.

WITH WELLINGTON'S LIGHT CAVALRY *by William Tomkinson*—The Experiences of an officer of the 16th Light Dragoons in the Peninsular and Waterloo campaigns of the Napoleonic Wars.

SERGEANT BOURGOGNE *by Adrien Bourgogne*—With Napoleon's Imperial Guard in the Russian Campaign and on the Retreat from Moscow 1812 - 13.

SURTEES OF THE 95TH (RIFLES) *by William Surtees*—A Soldier of the 95th (Rifles) in the Peninsular campaign of the Napoleonic Wars.

SWORDS OF HONOUR *by Henry Newbolt & Stanley L. Wood*—The Careers of Six Outstanding Officers from the Napoleonic Wars, the Wars for India and the American Civil War.

ENSIGN BELL IN THE PENINSULAR WAR *by George Bell*—The Experiences of a young British Soldier of the 34th Regiment 'The Cumberland Gentlemen' in the Napoleonic wars.

HUSSAR IN WINTER *by Alexander Gordon*—A British Cavalry Officer during the retreat to Corunna in the Peninsular campaign of the Napoleonic Wars.

THE COMPLEAT RIFLEMAN HARRIS *by Benjamin Harris as told to and transcribed by Captain Henry Curling, 52nd Regt. of Foot*—The adventures of a soldier of the 95th (Rifles) during the Peninsular Campaign of the Napoleonic Wars.

THE ADVENTURES OF A LIGHT DRAGOON *by George Farmer & G.R. Gleig*—A cavalryman during the Peninsular & Waterloo Campaigns, in captivity & at the siege of Bhurtpore, India.

LEONAUR

ALSO FROM LEONAUR
AVAILABLE IN SOFTCOVER OR HARDCOVER WITH DUST JACKET

LIFE IN THE ARMY OF NORTHERN VIRGINIA *by Carlton McCarthy*—The Observations of a Confederate Artilleryman of Cutshaw's Battalion During the American Civil War 1861-1865.

HISTORY OF THE CAVALRY OF THE ARMY OF THE POTOMAC *by Charles D. Rhodes*—Including Pope's Army of Virginia and the Cavalry Operations in West Virginia During the American Civil War.

CAMP-FIRE AND COTTON-FIELD *by Thomas W. Knox*—A New York Herald Correspondent's View of the American Civil War.

SERGEANT STILLWELL *by Leander Stillwell* —The Experiences of a Union Army Soldier of the 61st Illinois Infantry During the American Civil War.

STONEWALL'S CANNONEER *by Edward A. Moore*—Experiences with the Rockbridge Artillery, Confederate Army of Northern Virginia, During the American Civil War.

THE SIXTH CORPS *by George Stevens*—The Army of the Potomac, Union Army, During the American Civil War.

THE RAILROAD RAIDERS *by William Pittenger*—An Ohio Volunteers Recollections of the Andrews Raid to Disrupt the Confederate Railroad in Georgia During the American Civil War.

CITIZEN SOLDIER *by John Beatty*—An Account of the American Civil War by a Union Infantry Officer of Ohio Volunteers Who Became a Brigadier General.

COX: PERSONAL RECOLLECTIONS OF THE CIVIL WAR--VOLUME 1 *by Jacob Dolson Cox*—West Virginia, Kanawha Valley, Gauley Bridge, Cotton Mountain, South Mountain, Antietam, the Morgan Raid & the East Tennessee Campaign.

COX: PERSONAL RECOLLECTIONS OF THE CIVIL WAR--VOLUME 2 *by Jacob Dolson Cox*—Siege of Knoxville, East Tennessee, Atlanta Campaign, the Nashville Campaign & the North Carolina Campaign.

KERSHAW'S BRIGADE VOLUME 1 *by D. Augustus Dickert*—Manassas, Seven Pines, Sharpsburg (Antietam), Fredricksburg, Chancellorsville, Gettysburg, Chickamauga, Chattanooga, Fort Sanders & Bean Station.

KERSHAW'S BRIGADE VOLUME 2 *by D. Augustus Dickert*—At the wilderness, Cold Harbour, Petersburg, The Shenandoah Valley and Cedar Creek..

LEONAUR

ALSO FROM LEONAUR
AVAILABLE IN SOFTCOVER OR HARDCOVER WITH DUST JACKET

THE RELUCTANT REBEL *by William G. Stevenson*—A young Kentuckian's experiences in the Confederate Infantry & Cavalry during the American Civil War..

BOOTS AND SADDLES *by Elizabeth B. Custer*—The experiences of General Custer's Wife on the Western Plains.

FANNIE BEERS' CIVIL WAR *by Fannie A. Beers*—A Confederate Lady's Experiences of Nursing During the Campaigns & Battles of the American Civil War.

LADY SALE'S AFGHANISTAN *by Florentia Sale*—An Indomitable Victorian Lady's Account of the Retreat from Kabul During the First Afghan War.

THE TWO WARS OF MRS DUBERLY *by Frances Isabella Duberly*—An Intrepid Victorian Lady's Experience of the Crimea and Indian Mutiny.

THE REBELLIOUS DUCHESS *by Paul F. S. Dermoncourt*—The Adventures of the Duchess of Berri and Her Attempt to Overthrow French Monarchy.

LADIES OF WATERLOO *by Charlotte A. Eaton, Magdalene de Lancey & Juana Smith*—The Experiences of Three Women During the Campaign of 1815: Waterloo Days by Charlotte A. Eaton, A Week at Waterloo by Magdalene de Lancey & Juana's Story by Juana Smith.

TWO YEARS BEFORE THE MAST *by Richard Henry Dana. Jr.*—The account of one young man's experiences serving on board a sailing brig—the Penelope—bound for California, between the years 1834-36.

A SAILOR OF KING GEORGE *by Frederick Hoffman*—From Midshipman to Captain—Recollections of War at Sea in the Napoleonic Age 1793-1815.

LORDS OF THE SEA *by A. T. Mahan*—Great Captains of the Royal Navy During the Age of Sail.

COGGESHALL'S VOYAGES: VOLUME 1 *by George Coggeshall*—The Recollections of an American Schooner Captain.

COGGESHALL'S VOYAGES: VOLUME 2 *by George Coggeshall*—The Recollections of an American Schooner Captain.

TWILIGHT OF EMPIRE *by Sir Thomas Ussher & Sir George Cockburn*—Two accounts of Napoleon's Journeys in Exile to Elba and St. Helena: Narrative of Events by Sir Thomas Ussher & Napoleon's Last Voyage: Extract of a diary by Sir George Cockburn.

www.ingramcontent.com/pod-product-compliance
Lightning Source LLC
LaVergne TN
LVHW011400080426
835511LV00005B/366